ADHD, A Heartful Approach

Navigating ADHD
with less guilt, shame,
more talents and abilities

by Shane Bruce
the ADHD Guy
www.ADHDguy.com

Acknowledgements

I want to first acknowledge Diana Ferrari for helping me to realize I have ADHD. I want to also thank acting ACO (ADHD Coaches Organization) President, Jodi Sleeper-Triplett, for her mentoring, fellow ACO members, Evan Kirstein, Darrin Lee, and Ana Coppola. I want to thank David Giwerc, founder of ADD Coach Academy, and ADDCA Faculty, Barbara Luther. I want to thank my coach Dave Mochel of Applied Attention. I want to thank my readers and editors, Shaun Sanders, Phoenix Hocking, Caroline Meyer, Michaela Gordon, and Dr. Roland Rotz. Fianlly I want to thank Caroline Meyer for her bio photo and cover design concept, and Marc Borzelleca for his layout and design work.

To all the ADHDers and families I have worked with over the years: this book is for you.

Shane

ADHD, A HEARTFUL APPROACH

Introduction

"Why another book on ADHD?" a colleague, asked over coffee. That's a good question, I thought. There are already so many books on ADHD. Why this one?

The answer is easy. Since 1987 ADHD has been a thought of as a mental illness treated primarily with stimulant medication. But what if you wanted to try and live well with ADHD without meds? Are medications really the answer? What if even with the meds you still struggled in certain areas?

I came to an awareness of ADHD late in the game. I was lucky enough to find my own way and work in my strengths for the first half of my life. Ironically it was in entering the mental health field that I discovered what are called, "functional impairments." It was here that I was shamed and stigmatized, demoralized, and dehumanized by the established systems that hold the mental health field in our culture. But instead of accepting victimization, I did what most ADHDers do. I created a system to help me. I then tried this system out on others with ADHD and it seems to help them as well.

I found success with an empathic, heart-centered, and strengths based approach. Though combining different approaches that range from challenging stigma, bolstering self-efficacy, to somatic body-centered work, I was able to carve out the ability overcome basic characteristics that are associated with ADHD. I was able to increase my focus on what's important, manage my incredible kinetic hyperactivity, and re-direct impulses naturally, without feeling bad about myself.

I learned the most important thing is to practice loving-kindness – first toward myself, then toward others. Of course, a heart-centered approach does not just help with ADHD, it helps many other conditions as well. But for those of us with ADHD, who have suffered with toxic shame - being criticized, berated, and demoralized - because our strength set does not conform with the standards of the world around us, this book is for us! It's also for your parents, care-givers, teachers, administrators, and friends. So, come along on a journey that can potentially turn your functional impairments in to Superpowers!

ADHD, A HEARTFUL APPROACH

CONTENTS

1   **Shame Blame Game** **11**
    Shame 13
    Challenging the Stigma....................................... 17
    Who Cares.. 18
    Medication Remix...20
    Advocacy, Accommodation, and Action................... 21
    Healing the Shame That Binds Us................ 23
    KEY POINTS 24

2   **Heartful Meaning**... **25**
    KEY POINTS 27

3   **Strengths Chat** **29**
    Kohut's TriPoar Self..30
    You Are the Expert in YOU 31
    Context is Everything....................................... 32
    Show Me the Evidence 33
    KEY POINTS 35

4   **Values Compass** **37**
    Where Does the Time Go 37
    Multitasking Is An Illusion.............................. 38
    Time Studies.. 39
    The Role of Values... 41
    The Self Center 42
    Internal Commitments...................................... 43
    Four Quadrants for Optimal Living 44
    Scaling Our Stress 45
    Quadrant One: Sleep.. 45
    Quadrant Two: Eat 46
    Quadrant Three: Move...................................... 46
    Quadrant Four: Keep Good Company...................... 47
    KEY POINTS 48

5   **Heartfulness**... **49**
    What We Feel Others See................................50
    Anxiety and ADHD..50
    Depression and ADHD....................................... 52
    Energy Managements 54
    KEY POINTS 55

6   **Autopilot** **57**
    Tools for Reprogramming Unhelpful Beliefs............ 59
    KEY POINTS 60

7 Mindfulness **61**
I Feel, Therefore I Think, Therefore I Do 61
Feelings Are Not Facts 63
I Think, Therefore, I, huh 64
You Are What You Do 65
Making Believe 67
Rethinking Positive Thinking 68
Thinking May Save the World 69
Motivation and Willpower - Why-Flyin' 69
Tools for Grounding 70
KEY POINTS 71

8 Context is Everything! **73**
Light 75
Sound 76
Emotional Stress 77
Relational Environment 78
Food, Fitness, and Finance 80
My Lived Experience 81
Tools and Takeaways 83
KEY POINTS 84

9 Play it Again, Sam! **85**
Fragile Confidence 85
More Lived Experience 86
Radical Acceptance 87
Change 87
KEY POINTS 89

10 From Hateful to Heartful **91**
KEY POINTS 97

CHAPTER ONE

Shame Blame Game

Attention Deficit Disorder, better known as ADD was invented in 1980 by Dr. Virginia Douglas. Prior to this it was called *Minimal Brain Dysfunction.* In 1987 hyperactivity was added, and ADD became ADHD, where it remains to this day. But *attention deficit* is not an accurate description of this condition. Most of us with ADHD have a Superpower called *hyper-focus.* This means we can focus for really long periods of time. So to call what we have *attention deficit* is...well, inaccurate. It might be better called *Keeping Our Cool Deficit.* Or, how about, *Keeping Track Of Time Deficit*? But to be honest I don't really like the term *deficit.* It's not helpful. It implies there's something wrong with us, that somehow we are deficient. While literally thousands of college kids who don't have ADHD have gotten a cognitive boost with the speedy drugs prescribed to us, those of us who really have this condition continue to be demoralized, shamed, and marginalized.

We get used to feeling *bad.* We seem to perform poorly, make bad choices, have bad judgment, and do bad things. Bad, bad, bad! Bad becomes the basis of our Self-concept. We blame ourselves for everything. If our ego isn't strong enough (it's hard to have ego strength when you feel like you are doing everything wrong), we blame everyone else. And other people blame us for all of the above. However, most of us excel in certain areas, like athletics, music, or abstract thinking. We are simply caught up in what I call The *Shame Blame Game.*

Let me know if any of this is familiar:

From the ADHDer:

> Heyyyyyy! So sorry I'm late (again!)
> Oops! Sorry I knocked the ____ over (again!)
> Yikes! I forgot the ____ again! Sorry!
> Oh no! I just blurted out ____! Sorry!

From the people around the ADHDer:
> Why can't you get up on time?
> You're late – again?
> You lost the ___ again??
> Why don't you return my calls?
> Did you go MIA again??
> Did you miss the ____? I sent you an email about it!
> Can't you just THINK before you say something??

People often blame the ADHDer for having a condition that neuroscience shows to be inherent and innate. Once aware, there are things we can do to adjust to our ADHD, but it is no more our fault than skin pigment or the structure of our bones. Just as we are genetically imbued with challenges – or attributes that, when mixed with the environment, lead to challenges – we are also genetically endowed with gifts. What we call ADHD comprises both. Many ADHDers are significantly gifted in some areas while challenged in others.

ADHD is rooted in a delay in the development of certain parts of the brain, what we can look at as the *growth brain*. While the signs and symptoms of ADHD may lie dormant for years, being stimulated by environmental stressors, the innate capacities remain the same. ADHDers have an innate condition that is as immutable as hair, eye, and skin color.

Since shame and blame are no strangers to us, it's important to point out that ADHD is not a behavioral or conduct disorder in the usual sense. Trying to make ADHDers feel bad about the symptoms of their condition just leads to further distress, anxiety, depression, demoralization, and consequently, what behavioral science calls - *increased functional impairment*, AKA – The BADS!

Shame

The dictionary defines shame as – *a painful feeling of humiliation or distress caused by a consciousness of wrong or foolish behavior*. It goes on to tag words like, *guilt, regret, embarrassment, dishonor,* and *disgrace*. This is a state of being that many who have this condition live in – almost constantly. Many ADHDers report living in a sort of perpetual state of feeling bad because of something that we have either done or have not done. We feel out of control. If we consider what we have learned about ADHD, this should come as no surprise.

It's important here to differentiate shame associated with normal moral development. The medical language came to equate morality with behavior. But ADHD should not be seen as a moral blank check that lets those who have it off the hook in terms of normal moral development, especially when most of us are trying to live effectively and cope with the condition. In fact, it's likely that most people have a variety of challenging conditions to live with. ADHD might be seen as a chronic but manageable condition, like diabetes.

This is not to make excuses for someone with what behavioral sciences calls a *conduct disorder*, someone who might be trying to hang their foibles on a neurobiological condition. The objective is two-fold. One is to provide effective, user-friendly tools that make living with ADHD more manageable, and the other is to deliberately and consciously bolster the ADHDer's self-concept.

Why bolster the self-concept? The ADHDer is often the class clown and the funniest person in the room, but don't be misled by this fool's gold narcissism: it's not real. It's a form of fragile confidence. It's likely that the clownish behavior is how the ADHDer masks embarrassment and pain around not being able to function normally. Just below the surface of that charm and bravado is quite likely a sense of never being enough. We're driven to try and cover up profound feelings of inadequacy, either by avoiding situations that might expose burgeoning insecurity, or by remaining in a safe zone that highlights just our strengths. Or we might try both. This can make for an imbalanced personal development, which will be reflected in the personality. Well-rounded development can elude us. But with careful scaffolding and support, we can begin to carefully cultivate those parts of the brain that are delayed in development. The ADHDer may also work around the brain areas that are not yet developed, as well as make use of the exponential development of talents, abilities and skills that comprise the flow state that inhabits our hyper-focus. More on that as a gateway toward the cultivation of Superpowers for the ADHDer later!

Because we ADHDers often don't fit in to the standard parameters of socially acceptable norms, we sometimes develop what mid-twentieth century philosopher Martin Buber called existential guilt, or existential shame. This is where a person feels that their very being is wrong. The BADS. If we don't meet the expectations of those around us for long enough, we begin to feel despondent and demoralized. This results from a prolonged experience of feeling that who we are and what we are is so radically wrong that our very being or existence must be a mistake: a missed-take, a take that is incorrect or should be done over and over until we get it right. But what if we're not designed that way? Why should a Ferrari try to be a Toyota?

What if we were built like a Ferrari with a V12 engine, with 800 horsepower, reeved to 8,500 rpms, with a Max torque of 530 pound-feet, all of it pushed to the rear wheels, able to go from zero to 60 mph in just 2.9 seconds, with a top speed of 211 mph? We might be designed to drive the autobahn, but we're stuck in traffic with a bunch of Toyota Corollas. This is how many ADHDers feel in standard environments. Not that there is anything wrong with a Toyota Corolla. They are built for durability, endurance, stability, and reliability. These are just not our strengths. Our strengths are speed, performance, and power.

It may be useful to question the appropriateness of what we call standardized environments in terms of the functionality of the ADHDer. If a congested downtown freeway is a normal standardized environment, then yes, the Ferrari may feel demoralized and out of place. Hans Christian Anderson's fable of the Ugly Duckling tells the story of a swan that does not know it's a swan until it finds other swans and comes to appreciate its nature and beauty. All the while that the swan thinks it's a duck, it just doesn't feel right, thinking there is something terribly wrong with it. Sound familiar?

Many ADHDers struggle with standardized school environments and large noisy classrooms. Many of us find standardized testing quite difficult. We may be better at essay questions, or even oral exams, rather than multiple-choice questions wherein concrete detail is stressed. Many ADHDers struggle with this kind of thing in both school and work environments. Many find work environments with cubicles and florescent lighting and constant interruptions challenging. On the other hand, some of us thrive in noisy chaotic environments such as restaurants, where thinking on our feet in a fast paced setting is valued. This may seem like a contradiction, but some ADHDers actually find the din of a loud and chaotic environment helpful. There are neurological reasons for this, which we will explore and unpack later.

A display of symptoms can lead the ADHDer into a sort of Orwellian nightmare; one where thought police invade in the form of angry parents, administrators, and "helpful" professionals who all try to get the ADHDer to fit in to standardized environments, not unlike a totalitarian super-state. I've sat in Individual Education Plan (IEP) meetings and watched painfully as the tone of the adults in the room becomes sharper while, simultaneously, the body language of the child with ADHD has them sinking deeper and deeper into despondence and despair, like a dark viscose liquid that slips down off the chair onto the floor to join it's Spiritual counterpart – pond scum.

Today's standardized education has its roots in the *factory model* of education. This approach was cultivated in England during the Victorian era to turn children into good little automatons, cogs in the great wheel of the workplace. Prior to that, learning happened in apprenticeships that placed learning in the context of the *relationship* between master of the trade and the student/intern/apprentice. Students learned by doing under the tutelage of the master.

Another educational model used in Europe was called gymnasium, where teachers gave oral exams, and students had to answer from their experiential understanding of how the concepts worked. These models stand in stark contrast to the current public school model of rote memorization of material that has no meaning for the student. Teach to the test. This is how funding is secured. Real learning has gone by the wayside. *No child left behind* turned into *most kids left behind*. Certainly those who learn by doing in the context of a positive relationship with their teachers were left in the dust, flailing, and medicated. That would be those of us with ADHD!

Education theorist Sugata Mitra mounted a computer in a wall of a small village in India, which he connected to the Internet. The children who encountered the computer not only taught themselves English so that they could navigate the Internet, they then used new tools discovered on the Internet to develop intellectually. It would appear this far more organic and effective way to learn beat sitting in a cold plastic chair under florescent lights for six hours a day. Who knew?

Well, apparently Maria Montessori and Rudolf Steiner, founder of the Waldorf Schools did. If only the individualized learning resources and philosophy of exploration used in these settings were available to all public school kids. Unfortunately most standardized educational settings do not have these kinds of resources, largely because it's much cheaper to just give the kids some speedy psychiatric meds. It's a win-win. Stable kids. Drug companies make bank. But what might be possible if free access to learning was provided by teachers who cared more about teaching than getting a paycheck? Turns out, thanks to the Internet, that learning is now available in little Johnny and little Janey's bedrooms. Problem is, there is no one telling them what's a real fact, and what's fake fact. Sound like a recipe for disaster? Stay tuned...

Recent studies have shown that taking kids and forcing them to sit still all day, medicating them, and punishing them if they can't sit still, is a really bad idea. Yet this is precisely what's going on in most standardized educational settings. There are all kinds of physiological reasons why kids need to get up from their seats run around.

Research has shown that there are focusing and feel good chemicals, (dopamine and serotonin) released during intense physical exercise. Human beings are physiologically designed to run around, get food, collapse in front of the fire in the cave, cook, eat, play music, talk in meaningful ways, connect with each other, and go to sleep. Forcing a child to face the Orwellian Education Factory is putting chains on the Spirit and shackles on the Soul of our children. While education visionaries such Rudolf Steiner, and Maria Montessori lit a light that provided a beacon of hope for how learning might best happen, most of our education institutions have disappointingly fallen short of what might be possible for learning centers. But the Internet is changing that, and faster than we might imagine.

Challenging the Stigma

Some years ago, I was summoned to the Human Resources office of a nonprofit mental health facility where I worked as a clinical supervisor. A therapist I supervised was told that she would face disciplinary action if she did not catch up with her case notes. In spite of numerous work plans, and what seemed a heroic effort on her part, including her working over sixty hours a week to try and catch up, she remained critically behind. She obtained a letter from her doctor requesting specific accommodations related in innate brain processing conditions. She was denied. She was told that if she could not meet the contractual obligations of her position, she'd lose her job. I might add that the contractual agreements had changed dramatically from the time she had first been hired. What was required of her now was not on the strength side of her skill set. She was a highly trained drama therapist with post-graduate certifications and credentials in her area of specialization.

Over the course of my twelve-year career in public mental health, the funding contracts came to require a level of documentation was that was for many, including me, impossible to keep up with. For some, especially those therapists with ADHD, it took longer to document a service, than to perform the service. This documentation is expected to be quantifiable, measuring the impact of the interventions used by clinicians in these setting, justifying to the funders that the therapeutic work is worthy of their continued support.

With the support of my boss, I was able to put together a plan that enabled the therapist to keep her job. But I was surprised by the inflexibility of the Human Resources department of this nonprofit. I found it ironic that an agency whose mission it is to provide compassionate care to children and families was so insensitive to the functional needs of its employees. Fortunately I found support for this from the administration. This prompted me to develop and provide an overview presentation of not just how to work with ADHD in the children we served, but how to work with it, in our adult coworkers. To the agency's credit, the presentation was supported and given to several departments.

It's still hotly debated as to whether or not ADHD is considered a "real" mental health condition. It is without debate, however, that it's called a *disorder* in the medical context. The term, disorder, is built into the name ADHD. It is listed in the mental health Diagnostic and Statistical Manual as a condition that impacts mental health, therefore the wellbeing and efficacy of the person who is "afflicted." ADHD is seen by the medical and scientific world as a childhood behavioral disorder, a learning disorder, a processing disorder, and a brain developmental disorder. Thought as to how or why ADHD has been created is notably absent. How did a condition that was called Minimal Brain Dysfunction that appeared in approximately 2% of the childhood population get turned into a mental illness that impacted one out of five boys in America? Yes, many more boys than girls were diagnosed.

It's fortunate that the Human Resources department of that organization, one so committed to serving the wellbeing of children was able to find a way to show employees the same compassion they show their clients, thanks to the advocacy of a few key administrators. It was not without the pushback of advocates who were unwilling to play the Shame Blame Game. We were able to point to the legitimate system barriers that stood in the way of highly gifted healers, who care deeply about the wellbeing of children, doing their jobs.

Stigma can be born of cultural bias and ignorance. We need to be careful not to have contempt prior to investigation. Unfortunately, many health conditions, and indeed disease itself is subject to stigmatization in our culture. It's usually as the result of facing the challenges associated with living with these conditions that our ignorance is necessarily obliterated. Certainly learning more about ADHD will help challenge any biases we may have against it. We still have a long way to go, but neuroscience illuminates the chemical composition of focus enabling us to learn more about how to live with this at times maddening condition.

Who cares

One of the chief characteristics of ADHD is low-frustration-tolerance. ADHD is by definition not accurate. We don't have a deficit of attention. We have trouble integrating the survival brain with the growth brain. Our survival brain, the part connected to intense emotion makes us more sensitive to the world around us and to our own feelings. We feel too much, then get overloaded and shut down. We're then seen as distracted, and impatient. It may seem easier to just give up. As a kid in the classroom, if we are not engaged by what's being presented, we give up because we have no idea how to cope with how our mind processes what we are experiencing. As adults with ADHD we might find ourselves in jobs that make no sense to us, or in relationships with supervisors, family members, or partners who don't understand us. When that happens, we check out. If being in the moment were intolerable, why would we want to be there? Why not check out?

If you have ADHD, the critical questions to ask yourself are these: what do I care about? What makes a thing worthwhile? What motivates me? How can I find and stay connected to what's meaningful? Connection with meaning produces neuro-chemicals that help us calm down and stay focused.

So how do we deal with the stress that comes from both inside and outside us? We might be upset because we lost our keys (again!), or because we are remembering something some-body said that pissed us off. We might also be upset because we don't feel well physically. How do we keep our cool? My dearly departed grandmother Vyola-Sybil would say, "Precious Darlin', just brew your self a cup of tea and set for a spell." Imbued with wisdom born of the ingenuity necessitated by being of twenti-eth century pioneer stock, she was chock full of colloquialisms. When I spent happy youthful summers on the family farm, she'd say, "Boy, you'll attract more bees with honey than with vinegar." No one was more adaptive and inventive than she was. Maybe she had ADHD. She certainly modeled how to cope well with it if she did.

Grandma Vy's wisdom may have some value to helping us cope with ADHD. She taught us that we need to be patient and persistent; that in order to get what we want, sometimes we need to finesse a bit. All of us in the twenty-first century Western culture may be a bit too entitled - entitled, but not necessarily empowered. Empowerment comes from recognizing that things are better now for humans than they have ever been in the his-tory of humanity. Empowerment is taking responsibility for who we are, where we are, and cultivating a willingness to work with what we have. Why should you care? Because you are worth caring for! If you believe in a Benevolent Presence in the Universe, recognize that you are worthwhile because you are, not because of what you do.

Sitting around moaning and complaining about how messed up things are, while slightly gratifying in the moment in a misery-loves-company sort of way, can keep us too long embedded in the *problem saturated story*. Oh sure! Wallow in it. Roll around in the self-pity until you are thoroughly done and ready to get on with life. Yes, having ADHD sucks at times, and certain tasks may be more challenging. But thankfully we live in an exciting time when neuroscience is helping us to better understand how our brains function optimally.

Steve Kotler and Jaime Wheal, in the *Hacker Nation Flow Genome Project*, are breaking the code on how to enhance human performance across the board by understanding the neuroscience of it. The implications of this for people with ADHD may be quite exciting. A new and brighter era, where we utilize our strengths and our hyper-focus capacities may be right around the corner.

Medication Remix

What role and toll has the pharmaceutical industry had in shaping ADHD? What relationship does the pharmaceutical industry have with scientists, doctors, and standardized educational settings? Alan Schwarts's book, *ADHD Nation* explores this in depth and detail. Many have mixed feelings about treating ADHD with stimulant medications. Some parents of kids with ADHD struggle ethically with the notion of medicating the developing brains of their children. Medical doctors have varying opinions on the issue, and it remains quite controversial. Statistics in the US vary from state to state in terms of the number of school-aged children diagnosed with ADHD. Statistics vary from nation to nation as well. One reason for this may be the medicating practices of treating physicians and psychiatrists, as well as what regulations and protocols are considered the norm in each state and/or country.

This mixed data can make discernment for parents difficult. We might explore treatment practices with a curious and open mind, being careful not to fall prey to peer pressure or conventional thinking. We may also want to question the value of shaming our school-aged children because of their inability to sit still for six hours a day under florescent lighting in a facility with dwindling Physical Education and artistic programs.

Advocacy, Accommodation, and Action

In 1973, Section 504 of The Rehabilitation Act and The American Disabilities Act (ADA) recognized ADHD as a legitimate disability. Therefore people with ADHD have a right to behavioral and environmental accommodation. Over the past fifteen years, I have participated in advocacy encouraging school district representatives, teachers, and administrators to support parents and assist kids articulate their needs for living and working with ADHD.

The Mental Health America Peer Support Services movement evolved out of the *Social Recovery Model*, in which the *Parent Partner* provides support for parents of children with ADHD. They do so, not as a professional expert, but as someone who has been through it. For example, someone who has a child with ADHD and has had success in navigating the various challenges associated with standardized academic settings can help others who face the same challenges.

Several years ago I sat in a dingy, sterile classroom with a fifteen year-old student who was a client of mine. The teachers and school administrators talked down at him, reviewing his perceived character defects with cold precision. The three teachers in attendance aligned with each other, using a harsh, condescending tone, and proceeded to shame him for not being able to sit still or complete his work on time. When I pointed out their condescending and shaming tone, I was accused of aligning with my client against the teachers. I was not permitted to meet with them again without the school principal being present. I learned from this experience that sometimes being an agent of change is threatening to the status quo. I had pointed out that when they would not allow my client to use headphones that helped him concentrate, and would not permit him to take breaks when needed, they were violating his rights per the ADA. Further, the school held multiple classes in the same space at the same time under life-sucking florescent lighting that must have been manufactured by the Dementors from the Harry Potter books. When I pointed out that having multiple classes in the same space may add to the distractibility of my client, I was met by deeply entrenched system barriers in the form of school budget cuts and lack of space availability.

Although I underwent the painful realization that I was not going to change the Los Angeles Unified Public School's policies in that moment, I was able to advocate for my client to attend a different school with smaller classes, and with more of an individualized academic program. While I may have offended teachers and administrators who were deeply invested in the old broken systems, I was able to model for my client, coaching him in not accepting the unacceptable. This is as opposed to quietly suffering in shame, accepting blame for a condition that he did not ask for, or for "bearing up" under the brunt of an education system that just doesn't work for kids with ADHD.

The key to initiating action, advocacy, and accommodation is to ask for what you need. When the time comes to take action, just take the next indicated step. Don't let fear and discouragement render you paralyzed. So many people with ADHD are demoralized by their existential shame. When that dark amorphous cloud descends upon us and attaches itself to our energetic field like an amoebic blob, it's time to take action; any action initiating self care, such as getting up out of bed, taking a shower, going for a walk, run, or bike ride. Or even calling a supportive friend or family member can help.

The Latin root for courage is *cor*. Cor means *heart*. Take heart! And in spite of feeling shame, doubt, and fear, pick our selves up, dust our selves off, and move forward. Eastern philosophy can help us here. The Buddhists say: "If you fall, get up. If you fall again, get up again." Always keep the beginner's mind. Taoist philosopher, Lao Tzu, reminds us that the journey of a thousand miles begins with the first step.

Once you have taken action, the next step is to become armed with information. Learn more about ADHD. There are many resources listed in the back of this book where you can garner basic information about the condition. Once you have information, educate others around you. We call this *psycho-education* because it means learning more about brain function and the impact of that function on our thinking, feelings, and behaviors. The term psyche is associated with mind, and since ADHD is a brain condition, it affects the mind. Helping others to learn about the condition can reinforce and legitimize what we already know, enabling such knowledge to sink in. Hearing ourselves articulate our experience can help with our own metacognition.

Finally, explore the need for accommodation. We might need time to take standardized tests, or completing certain types of assignments. We often qualify for other types of ADA accommodation, such as talk-to-text technology in the workplace. Make determinations as to what is the best kind of accommodation for you, or the ADHDer you care for.

Healing the Shame That Binds Us

For ADHDers, healing that shame that binds must begin with a strengths-chat, focusing on what we have already done well. Most ADHDers are exceptional in some areas while severely challenged in others, which can result in a fractured self-concept. Many lose sight of their strengths, drowning in the demoralizing emphasis of our inability to function "normally." Being reminded of what we are good at helps. Brian Johnson, in his online *Optimal Living* programs, points out that for every one negative criticism, we need ten compliments. He says that positive feedback is like Teflon, it just bounces off, while negative criticism is like Velcro – it locks on and holds. The reason for this is that our ancient brain – what is sometimes is called the *reptilian brain* – once needed to ruminate about the negative in order to survive. The fight-flight-freeze mechanism associated with the baser brain holds on to the negative, while the stories told about our accomplishments and abilities seem to just roll off, like water off Teflon.

Through gaining an understanding of the Self through looking at our talents, abilities, interests, and values, we can develop a sense of efficacy. ADHD presents a unique set of demands that make developing and sustaining that efficacy a little more challenging. This is where a strengths-chat and a focus on what a person has to offer can begin to provide a foundation for healing existential shame.

KEY POINTS

- Shame versus guilt – guilt is feeling bad about something we do whereas shame is feeling bad about who we are; our innate qualities.

- Ferrari's and Toyota's – helping the ADHDer recognize that they may have extraordinary gifts that can balance out the areas that need development.

- Challenging the Factory Model of Education and why that model usually doesn't work for the ADHDer.

- How to bounce back and build resiliency against existential shame.

- The medication remix – to medicate or not to medicate; be discerning.

- The Triple A Threat: Advocacy, Accommodation, and Action.

- Healing the shame that binds – how do we get past the shame associated with feeling less-than because we have ADHD.

CHAPTER TWO

Heartful Meaning

It became clear that whether we have ADHD or not, we need to live more meaningful lives. For those of us with ADHD this is not a luxury. This is crucial.

For us it's essential to connect with who we really are. Whether we are artists, business people, housewives, magicians, entomologists, professional surfers, teachers, or students, we have to focus on being our Authentic Selves. But how? I have outlined a five (5) point system to help.

1. **Strengths Chat -** Starting with what I call the *Strengths Chat*, we highlight what we're good at and find evidence of it. We then keep that evidence up front and center.

2. **Values Compass -** Next we do what has historically been called the *Time Study*, or a Time Audit, a practice often used in Executive Coaching. For our purposes, in addition to assessing how we spend our time, we quickly realize it is really a Values Audit. As time is an illusion, it is a construct created for us to cooperate.

3. **Self-Center -** Then we move on to what I cheekily call the *Self Center*. Using the primary colors of Red, Blue, and Yellow, we create a map of intention that expands into a flower, and ultimately a Mandala. Borrowing from C.G. Jung, we use the mandala as a representation of the Self. This then leads to an understanding of our Internal Commitments. Internal Commitments are the agreements we've made with ourrselfs.

4. **Heartfulness -** Next we come to the practice of *Heartfulness*, a very recent idea that stems from Eastern philosophies. While

Western psychology has run with Mindfulness, less emphasis has been placed on The Heart. The HeartMath Institute provides us with a context for exploring the central role that The Heart plays in our quest for integrated self-awareness. We explore how to process strong emotions in a way that can keep us clear and effective in our daily lives. For many of us living with ADHD, strong emotions are a significant challenge. Heartfulness may need to even come before the Strengths Chat. Finally, we examine and explore the ADHDers relationship with the environment, including other people. ADHD is a condition exacerbated by environmental stimuli, so paying close attention to how the ADHDer relates to the environment can make the difference between running for the hills and kicking back with a cool drink.

5. **Context** – Finally we look at the environment that the ADHDer is in. We look at environmental stimulation, such as light and sound. We explore the impact of stress as well as consider how eating habits and intense physical exercise impact ADHD. Close relationships are part of this as well. Do they enhance, diminish, or demoralize? Work and academic settings are assessed. We work not on changing the person with ADHD as much as finding a context that is right for us.

Are you ready? Let's get started.

KEY POINTS

- A Heartful approach can lead to a more meaningful life.

- The Strengths Chat – Highlighting our talents, abilities, and skills and putting them up-front and center, covered in depth in chapter 4.

- The Time Audit – looking at how we spend our time and determining what our values are, covered in depth in chapter 5.

- Developing a map of intention called the Self Center to determine what's important to the ADHDer, and come up with strategies for making sure those things are taken care of, covered in depth in chapter 6.

- Internal commitments – once what's important is determined, a system for making sure that agreements the ADHDers make with themselves are done.

- Exploring how the ADHDer navigates and negotiates environmental and relationship stressors.

CHAPTER THREE

Strengths Chat

Inevitably, the proverbial poop will hit the fan. It's a given. In the first chapter we talked about the *Shame Blame Game*. The purpose of the *Strengths Chat* is to interrupt the shame blame game. Many of us living with ADHD have fumbled and bumbled our way through life, apologizing for being late, not making deadlines, losing this or that, saying things at the wrong time, and missing appointments. We are inclined to apologize for our mere existence. For many of us living with ADHD, this leads to low self-esteem and a poor self-concept.

The first step is to strengthen that sense of self by emphasizing the positive aspects of the Self. Noted mid-twentieth century psychologist Heinz Kohut provides us with an understanding of how the Self is structured. He was the first to map the Self out in a way that's easy to understand. Kohut's *Tri-Polar Self* offers an opportunity to identify and explore our talents, skills, ambitions, ideals, and values. The Strengths Chat does just that. Assessing talents, abilities, values, and ideals helps us to understand who we are. Then, exploring how these talents and abilities have been applied in context is crucial. Stimulation from the environment and our relationships with other people factor in with how the Self develops and is expressed.

Kohut's TriPolar Self

This Tri-Polar Self consisted of three vital qualities:

- Ambition/Striving
- Ideals/Values
- Talents/Skills

It may seem a paradox that while the Self is an independent entity it is constantly in a relationship with the world around it, one that includes both internal and external stressors. A resilient Self is essential to living meaningfully with ADHD. But in building a stronger *We* – whether that *We* is a partnership of two, a family, or part of a larger global community – it can only be as strong as the individual parts, the individual Selves that make up the whole. So, tending to the Self is essential to healthy partnerships, groups, organizations, nations, and the world at large.

Kohut pointed out how invaluable empathy is to healing the wounded Self. Empathy can come from outside ourselves from a loving parent, spouse or mentor, but it can also be cultivated within us, toward ourselves. This is reflective of the Buddhist idea of the Compassionate Witness, wherein we give ourselves the same loving kindness that we usually reserve solely for others. For those with ADHD, the value of this can be crucial, given the stigma and shame associated with ADHD. We live in a world that's very hard on us. Most of us have a pretty lame self-concept. Others might say to us, "Yeah, man, I get it! I've been where you're at!" Their experience and support can be a model for how we learn to treat ourselves.

For those of us with ADHD, when we give ourselves empathy, we make allowances for ourselves, and from our own experiences. No one can take that away from us, nor tell us that our experience is wrong. Only we can make that determination. In chapters to come, we'll explore in more depth how *relationships* influence our sense of self, and we'll look at the role relationships play in living meaningfully with ADHD. But for now, let's keep our focus on the Self and our strengths.

How, then, do we do that? First, we make a list of all the things we are good at. Next, we make a list of others who recognize these traits. This could be parents, siblings, co-workers, teachers, or counselors - anyone in our lives who have reflected our best traits back to us or brings out what is best in us. What were the conditions that brought out the best in us? How did we manifest these talents, skills, ideals, and values? What are our strengths? Why are they hard to talk about? We might think it's too egotistical or boastful to talk about our strengths, yet in a job interview, we are asked to do just that. The group we are interviewing for wants to know what we bring to the table. So, before our next interview, the Strengths Chat is a chance for us to gain insight and clarity about what we have going for us.

Strengths are reflected in the ideas we have about ourselves: how we think about ourselves. These thoughts are formed in words. Later, we will explore in depth the relationship between thoughts, feelings, and actions. For now, let's touch on the power of thoughts and words. Words carry a tremendous amount of power. Considering the words we use to describe ourselves is important. We will need to use words to describe our strengths.

In her novel, *The Thirteenth Tale*, Diane Setterfield pays homage to the power of words. She points out that words can take us prisoner. She poetically describes that way words can infect our minds and then influence our feeling states. She likens this to a kind of magic depicting how words an influence the unconscious mind without our being aware of it.

You Are the Expert in YOU

The Strengths Chat comes from something called *Brief Solution Focused Therapy*, which uses a here-and-now approach. In the Solution Focused model there is an assumption that instead of the professional being the expert, we are the experts on ourselves. Typically, the expert could be a doctor, a psychotherapist, or an ADHD coach. But we know ourselves better than anyone else, and our knowledge and interpretation of our strengths is what really matters. This represents a paradigmatic shift from the traditional way of seeing things, wherein the "expert" knew what was best for you. It represents a more collaborative approach.

The *Values In Action* or *VIA Survey* is an excellent way to assess strengths. Based on Martin Seligman's work with positive psychology, the strength survey is a fast way to identify our character virtues and give us a dashboard to keep them at the ready, and at the quick. Of course there are other surveys, such as the Gallop Poll that can also do this, but the VIA is free and fairly short, making it more manageable for those of us with ADHD. You can discover it by visiting the VIA Character website.

Still another strengths model comes from the recovery movement. The idea is that folks who are living with conditions such as addiction or ADHD can use the wisdom of their lived experience to help others. The model focuses on resiliency in the face of adversity and takes a holistic approach. This model states:

Strength-based assessment is defined as the measurement of those emotional and behavioral skills, competencies, and characteristics that create a sense of personal accomplishment, contribute to satisfying relationships with family and peers, and enhance one's ability to deal with adversity and stress, and promote one's personal, social and academic development.

Context is Everything

This idea is so important we've added a whole chapter devoted to it later. Most ADHDers are really good at some things, and really bad at others. Most of us live in a world of extreme opposites. For example, Sean is a world-class martial artist. He has been written up in trade magazines and is sought after worldwide because of his extraordinary skills. He came to me because he wanted to complete his college degree but could not function in a community college setting. He had made several attempts, with discouraging results that led to a downward spiral and a severe bout of depression. All he wanted to do was pass one class in community college. Sounds simple, right?

In spite of being able to grasp the central ideas in the class, he would tune out during class lectures and discussions. He was always late. He would frequently miss class. He would then get so far behind the curve that he could not catch up, and he ultimately failed the class

Together we talked about what is necessary to succeed in this particular context. We talked about how quickly he processes information, and how he views standardized education as largely a waste of time. When I asked him why, he said, "Because so much emphasis is placed on things that don't matter." I pointed out that this might be true, but that he had set this goal for a reason, and it was important that he realize the reason was his own. Sean had struck out on the first key to any endeavor: motivation. If you don't buy in, you don't have anything.

Show Me the Evidence

I asked Sean why he wanted to take a community college class. He told me it was to prove he could do it. Sean was already an elite athlete, and when I asked him what evidence he had of this, he told me of the many trophies he'd won in competitions that were packed away, buried in the closet. I encouraged him to unpack those trophies and dust them off, then proudly display them in a prominent place in his environment. That way, he could see evidence of his competencies on a regular basis. We analyzed strengths that he already had to help him move past the barriers to functioning in a conventional academic setting.

So what are you good at? I want you to really think about this. You don't need to be a world-class athlete.

When Lucy came to see me, she had a really hard time identifying anything that she was good at. She couldn't think of a single thing. So I asked her to get feedback from people who know her. She asked her parents, co-workers, and boyfriend to identify and reflect her strengths back to her. In an email, her parents identified characteristics such as "good with children," and "good with animals," among others. For Lucy, it was not as simple as going to the closet and dusting off trophies for display. How would she evidence "good with animals?" How would she make concrete the statement, "I am good with animals, as evidenced by...?"

I asked Lucy to go to the store and buy a corkboard and push pins. I then suggested she have her boyfriend take a photo of her petting her dog, print it out, and put the picture up on the cork board. I encouraged her to do this with each of the strengths that her parents had included in the email, things such as, "good with organization," and "good at organizing her house." I pointed out that by taking pictures, or writing down verbatim what others said she was good at, then posting those items on her corkboard, she had produced evidence of her strengths. She could then hang the corkboard somewhere in plain sight where she could look at it regularly, and most importantly, at times when she was not feeling good about herself.

Here, the role of the coach is that of collaborator, cheerleader for change and exception, elicitor of client strengths, resources, and competencies.

Here are a few concrete exercises:

List five things you are good at.

Ask a person close to you list five things you are good at.

See if there are any matches.

List the top three.

Find concrete evidence of those three (for example, a photograph, a written statement such as the one above, or an award, trophy, or anything that can reflect the statement, "I am good at _____ as evidenced by_____."

Next, find a surface that is easily seen in your personal space. It can be a white board, bulletin board, the front of the refrigerator, or closet door in your bedroom. It might be a small side table or shelf, or other display surface. Place the evidence of what you rock at in that space. So, when that proverbial poop hits the fan, as it inevitably will, we can look upon this area of competency with confidence and remember that in certain areas, we are Rock Stars! This can combat the negative perception of ourselves that stops us when we feel totally buried by the downside of having ADHD.

KEY POINTS

- Heinz Kohut lays out the anatomy of the Self giving us an understanding of what we are made of, our talents, abilities, values, and ambitions.

- Empathy – it's easy to have for others but not so easy to cultivate toward ourselves, especially when we are beating ourselves up for saying this, or not doing that!

- The power of words – Diane Setterfield in her novel *The Thirteenth Tale* depicts how much power words have over our experience and feeling state.

- You are the expert in YOU! Rather than relying on a Professional assessment of you, no one can tell you that your experience is wrong. The recovery movement emphasizes the value of lived experience in helping others.

- Context is everything! What you are doing, where, with whom, and how can make all the difference in how well or not well you function.

- What are you good at? The Strengths Chat is designed to help us focus on what we are good at. It's important to find evidence of that and keep it visible on a regular basis.

CHAPTER FOUR

Values Compass

Where Does the Time Go

"Wha...? Oh no! I lost track of time...Again!"

If I had a dollar for every time an ADHDer told me they'd lost track of time, I'd be buying a small island in the South Pacific. The refrain goes something like this: "I don't know what happened! The time just got away from me again. I set timers, and wrote sticky notes! I drew stuff on my arm! I had someone call me. I even laid all my clothes out and put my keys, wallet, and phone right by the door, and still I was late! What is wrong with me?" Secretly, inside, I think if we really tried, we could be on time. Am I kidding myself, and being unduly critical? Can people with ADHD really not help being late? Are we doomed, forever destined to temporal inability?

I've been lost in time wormholes on more occasions than I'd care to admit. It invariably leads to embarrassing apologies to whoever was waiting for me. I have to try and rationalize or justify being late for the umpteenth time. But invariably I realize, I haven't a leg to stand on. My behavior sends a message that they are not really that important to me. It makes them feel like I value whatever I was doing more than I value them. I feel like a heel trying to explain that is not the case. I feel like they don't believe me, and think I'm a jerk, not taking them seriously, that I'm immature, or just plain careless, a bad person. Inside I can feel myself trying to defend that poor little part of me that feels totally out of control. Once again, the Shame Blame Game has me in its grip.

I've concluded that it's *always later than we think*. When I do get into the habit of checking the time, I'm always astounded by how much more quickly the time is passing that I thought it was. It would seem that there is never as much time as we think there is. Of course this has global and philosophical implications. How often do we think about how precious these living present moments are? Do we realize that time is passing us by at an astonishing rate? One day we might wake up and exclaim Holy Mountains of digital clocks! Where did the time go?

But it's even more Twilight-Zonish than that. Time, such as we use it is rooted to geography. When I Skype my brother in Japan it is the future where he is. My 3pm today is his 7am tomorrow. Without going too far down a metaphysical wormhole, it's worth noting the subjective nature of time. Although loosely based on the rhythms of the planet, time, such as we've come to know it is largely as a human-constructed system used in Western cultures to co-operate.

I've attended Indigenous ceremonies where the social and cultural regard for time was quite different than what we're used to. Indigenous cultures are rooted more in the cycles of nature, such as seasons and phases of moon. They don't use devices such as clocks, watches, or satellites for telling time. The ceremony I attended had no regard for time as we conceive of it. The emphasis was on the quality of the event, more than how long it took to do. It was expected that participants would stay involved until the ceremony was complete, even if it went on all night.

This represents a very different way of viewing time, one that might shed light on ways of being that are different from the values of our culture. Many ADHDers have strengths in areas that are more in step with natural and indigenous cycles and cultures. Breakthroughs in both art and science often require stepping out of the usual ways of seeing things. Many people with ADHD are quite creative because the ADHD brain does process differently. Seeing things differently can provide value in terms of identifying previously unidentified solutions. The ADHDer can often put things together in ways not conventionally thought of. This shift in perspective can be vital to the ADHDer discovering ways to be efficacious because their brains work differently.

Multitasking Is An Illusion

It would seem that living in today's vastly complex world requires a Master's degree in Time Management. When I first

entered the workplace, the idea of going above and beyond had
not yet become an expectation. Workers focused on one thing
at a time. Now, multi-tasking is expected in most settings. The
non-stop barrage of emails and texts is enough to drive anyone to
anxiety. She or he who "manages" their time best, and is able to
juggle five or six tasks simultaneously is most valued. While the
ADHDer can appear to multitask, even thrive on overstimulation,
this is potentially a recipe for disaster for many of us.

It's been well documented that multi-tasking is impossible.
The brain is not capable of focusing on more than one thing at
a time. Doing so is an illusion, and is done best by people who
can transition quickly from one area of focus to another. There
may seem to be an aptitude for such ability amongst those with
ADHD because we have had to be fast responders out of neces-
sity and survival. Adrenaline is our friend. But we may have
missed the key points in any communication, and we're fast on
our feet because we're probably trying to "fake it till we make it."
Many of us make good sales people, with often seemingly manic
and sometimes charismatic personalities, which are really just
adaptive measures for masking the sheer terror and feelings of inadequacy that we feel when we don't know what's going on. We
don't do well with transitions of focus. It's during transitions that
we are most easily distracted. That's when we go down the rabbit
hole, and time just slips away.

Time Studies

The Time Study, or Time Audit is designed to help you find
your lost time. First, we need to go out and buy a planner. I use a
daily planner that breaks the day down into fifteen-minute seg-
ments. Yes, this is the old fashioned type we used before calendars
went electronic. Sure, go ahead and use Google Calendar or iCal
for important events you want to be alerted to, but for schedul-
ing, use that daily planner, a pencil, and a large eraser. Keep the
planner close to you at all times. Write in what you plan to do and
circle or outline the time allotted for the completion of our task.
This is a guestimate, not an actual measure of the time it will take;
base the time allotted on how long a similar task has taken you in
the past.

This is called *Time Budgeting*, and it is a useful habit. It can help us track *dead time* and *lost time*. This includes those endless hours spent on Facebook, Insta, Snap, or Twitter, or researching that thing-a-ma-jig, or that whatch-a-ma-call-it online. It helps answer that maddening question, *where did the time go?* We are shedding light on our actual habits and activities.

Since many of us have not really thought deeply about how we spend our time, this can be an enlightening exercise. We are essentially shedding light on what our actual values are. It's kind of taking inventory or running a cost analysis on how we spend our precious moments on Earth. It helps take look at what Jessica McCabe from *How To ADHD* calls activities that are too *time-spensive*. In 2007, Tim Ferris introduced the idea of *time affluence* in his book *The 4 Hour Work Week, Escape 9-5, Live Anywhere, and Join The New Rich*. Ferris highlights that time is our greatest resource, and how we spend it says a lot about who we are, essentially pointing out that in the digital age we can spend less time working in jobs that are meaningless and unfulfilling to us, and more time pursing our real passions.

While this is but one component of what a heart centered approach to ADHD is designed to help you do, if we are not enjoying the time that we are *not working*, then what kind of quality-of-life do we really have? The ideas and tools outlined in this book are designed to go beyond just time affluence to something I call *experiential affluence.*

I recommend using an analogue time tracking system. Although I recommend a time tracking system that measures down to 15-minute increments, we don't need to get too specific. We'll do that later when we develop what I call the *Self Center*. There are a plethora of analog notebooks and planners available online that can serve this purpose, or you can use the Time Study diagram. I recommend using a pencil and a big eraser. First we want to circle the time and write out what we have planned in pencil. Don't worry – we'll reconcile it later once we've actually done things. We can use our electronic calendars as a springboard for entering planned activities. Then, at the end of the day we reconcile so we can see what we actually did. It's best to do this daily, as it's easy to forget what we did if we fall too far behind. While this might seem cumbersome, I only recommend doing this for three weeks. Audits don't last forever! Do it at a time when the study will reflect a pretty typical couple of weeks. In other words, not during the holidays, nor when on vacation. We want an accurate picture of our normal lives.

Next - with red, blue, and yellow markers, we are going to divide our time into three categories – work, personal, and social. This color-coding uses primary colors for a reason. Later we'll examine where our activities overlap. We'll make purple, green, and orange. But for now let's keep it simple, sticking to the three categories and the three primary colors.

By increasing awareness of how time is spent, we have a better idea of what we are actually doing. This tells us what our actual values are, and what we are doing that accounts for our lost time. By writing down what we do, we become aware of how we actually spend time. This can highlight any discrepancy between what we are doing and what we want to do. Now we can see what our real values are.

The Role of Values

In earlier chapters we talked about strengths. Our strengths are often associated with our values. However, we are not always aware of what our values are. Our values have everything to do with how we spend our time. Our actions and behaviors are the walking waking measure of our values. Some say time is really the only commodity we have. You could be a 99-year-old billionaire who is out of time. We have not yet developed the technology to procure biological immortality, or reverse the aging process. At least not yet! So, no amount of money can buy time back. But I say how we capitalize on the energy we have in this moment is our true commodity. We focus on what we value.

It's worth repeating. How we spend our time tells us everything about who we are and what our values are. Values are linked to motivation. Most ADHDers are not going to do anything they don't really want to do. So, if you say that one of your values is to save the whales, I would ask where in your time budget is the whale saving showing up? Have you sewn it in to the fabric of your life plan? This external scaffold is crucial to what we call executive function. Planning and organizing is where we need bolstering. Most of us with ADHD need these external scaffolds on a regular basis. The Self Center can help provide that external scaffold.

The Self Center

We get easily distracted and lose track of what's important to us. In our time/values audit we were able to determine what is important to us. The *Self Center* can act as a dashboard to keep that focus up front and center. It can be especially meaningful for people who tend to be *others-centered*. We have been told that we should focus on others and put their needs before our own. In our culture this altruistic idea is considered noble. Caring for others is necessary. There may be times when sacrificing ourselves is indeed necessary. But abject altruism has led to a culture of co-dependency and a poor self- concept for many.

In the same way that placing the oxygen mask on yourself first before your children is necessary in a plane crash, how can you possibly be there for others if you are not clear about who you are and if you have not taken care of yourself? Charity begins at home. Muhammad Ali said, "If you don't stand up for yourself, who will?" Representing a healthy self-interest is not only okay it's necessary. So set aside your unselfish biases for a moment and focus on you!

Take a blank piece of paper, or a very large post-it and put it up on the wall. Now, draw a circle in the center and put your name or the word "Self" inside the circle. This is your Self Center! You are at the center of your map of intentions. Moving out from your Self Center, establish three (3) circles ○ ○ ○ that represent different aspects of the Self. They are:

○ Work - Red
○ Personal Care – Blue
○ Social - yellow

As you move out from your Self Center, establish the broad based categories outlined above, work, personal care, and social, each represented by primary colors. Red is for work and all things pertaining to money, including any training or schooling that you are doing that is preparing you to make money. For students, this would be school. Next draw a blue circle to represent personal care. This includes hygiene, fitness, shopping, and environmental care, such as house cleaning, laundry, etc. Finally a yellow circle will represent all things social. This includes friends, family, community, any volunteer work you might be doing, connection with

Spiritual organizations, such as church, etc. That is considered Tier One, or the first level of your Self Center.

Tier Two is where we get more specific. As you move away from the Self Center, become more and more specific about what it is exactly that you want to do. For example, you might have "Education" as a Tier Two broad category. Exactly what is it you want to do? Your map of intention might entail something like this:

- ○ Red: Education – Grad School – Send In Application
- ○ Red: Career – Find job closer to home – List Resume on Employment Website
- ○ Blue: Home – Paint Bathroom – Choose Color – Ask Son to Help
- ○ Yellow: Visit Aunt and Uncle and cousins.

These are just some samples. Make it fun, and colorful as well, by choosing a different color for each category that moves out form your Self Center.

Internal Commitments

From the Self Center we begin to get a sense of what it we think we want in order to be happy and fulfilled. This actually stimulates dopamine production, the focusing neurotransmitter! Again, a little fun helps keep things interesting. It can be really exciting to explore what we want, especially when we've been so focused on trying to change ourselves to fit in with the world around us. Many ADHDers have never been asked what they want. So it can be a little scary and disorienting for someone who is not used to even thinking about what they want. Similar to what happens in the Strengths Chat, it may be hard to determine what we want.

Often we discover that what we thought we wanted and what we really want are completely different. So often, what we think we want turns out to be what our parent's want, what our spouses want, or what our culture and society says we should want. The Self Center is designed to help us uncover our true desires and discover our authentic self. It's an opportunity to discard any and all false notions of Self that have been adopted along the way simply to please or appease others.

Next, we need to find a way to concretize our map of intentions in order to prepare for the idea of turning them into actionable items. I call this the forming of Internal Commitments. Why internal? They are internal because they come from within you, not from the outside world. THEY NEED TO MAKE SENSE AND HAVE MEANING TO YOU. What promises have you made to yourself? What did you say you were going to do? What's on your Bucket List, and what's on your Chuck-It List? When we look at the time audit, we will learn that this is really related to what your values are: our values are our internal commitments. This idea was borrowed from a yoga journal that used the example of paying rent or mortgage for sanctuary, pointing out that we spend time making money to pay rent or mortgage because we value having a home and a sanctuary.

Why commitment? Because intentions have been established on our map, and it is understood that barriers and challenges will rise in our quest to fulfill our Heart's Desires. So this process requires a steadfast stay-the-course kind of resolve. Later, we will discuss using the WOOP (wish, outcome, obstacle, plan) method to stay on course toward meeting our goals.

Contingencies are vital here. If Plan A doesn't work, then try Plan B. If Plan B is a no-go, we move on to Plan C. And so on. When we're driving, we always need to know alternate routes in case traffic is bad. In the same way, thinking through and planning for any challenges that might come up is our way of making and keeping our commitment to ourselves.

This requires that dreaded dratted word that sends us all running for the hills – discipline! Discipline is being a *disciple of the True Self*. We need to be disciples of our authentic selves. In doing this, we adhere to what our values are and keep that vision clear. If we can do this, we are well on our way to a more meaningful, fulfilling life.

The Four Quadrants For Optimal Living

The Four Quadrants for Optimal Living are Sleep, Eat, Move, and Good Relations. They are foundational in terms of helping us regulate our nervous systems and can keep our stress levels lower. While there are many techniques we can use in the moment to help stay cool, they might be considered reactive. But The Four Quadrants uses a proactive approach to treat distress. Whether ADHDer or Co-ADHDer, we all can benefit from paying attention to these foundational points for optimal living.

Scaling Our Stress

If you are operating normally at a lower distress level, when stressors happen you will handle them better. Paying close attention to the Four Quadrants can mean the difference between a 3 and a 6. As a baseline, if you were to scale stress from 0 to 10, imagine 0 being no stress at all and ten being so stressed you can't stand it. If you're walking around at a 6 all the time, adding 3 to it brings you up to a 9, which is almost intolerable. But if our baseline is a 3, adding 3 only brings you to a 6, making our ability to cope with the stressor much more effective.

Quadrant One: Sleep

Sleep is one of the most important components of health. Although the autonomic nervous system can run this bodily function without conscious input from us, we can control our sleep hygiene. Recent scientific inquiry shows that sleeping in a screen-free zone can be a very good idea. Many people now set a time of day or evening when they shut down their screens. Studies show a digital sunset two hours before bed is advisable. This includes cell phones, computers, and tablets, as well as television screens. Research shows that the blue light emitted from most screen-based devices can interrupt circadian rhythms, inhibit melatonin production, and contribute to a lack of cooling of the body at night. All of this inhibits sleep hygiene.

For people with ADHD, getting good sleep can be the difference between throwing a book at the wall in frustration because you are so overwhelmed by that stupid equation you've been working on for hours, or utilizing the BadAssed coping strategies our ADHD coach gave us, like planned fun and the use of humor. It's hard to laugh and have an angry outburst at the same time. Both activities release the pent up energy, but one is easier on the person and the world around them.

Getting a decent night's sleep can be the difference between really messing things up with friends, family, and co-workers, or dealing with conflict like the Rock Star that I know that you are!

Quadrant Two: Eat

Food is mood, and mood is a big thing for us ADHDers. A dip in our blood sugar can make the dramatic difference between whether we smile and wave, or scowl and mutter expletives under our breath at the ever-annoying next door neighbor who wants to talk at us endlessly while her dog barks incessantly. This, of course, goes for everyone, even you non-ADHDers. But for those with ADHD brains, what we eat, when we eat, and how we eat can be the difference between a severe depressive downward spiral and a day when we are doing the Snoopy dance.

Popular wisdom points toward the idea of keeping our blood sugar levels stable. The problem with refined sugars and starches is that they cause a spike in our blood sugar, leading to a severe dip, and ultimately a crash. This is why many kids with ADHD who have sugary cereals for breakfast are off the chain for the first hour at school, where they're unable to sit still. Then they crash and burn, collapsing into a lifeless clump that's unable to focus, pay attention, or get any work done. The same thing happens in the adult diet, where we're up and about for the first hour or so at work, bouncing from cubicle to cubicle, annoying and interrupting co-workers, regaling them with humorous anecdotes, then off to the snack cart in search of another sugary treat to take us through to lunch. But not without the crash and burn that leads to being about as productive as a lazy cat on a sunny summer afternoon. This, of course, leads to a write up from our supervisor and still more trouble with Human Resources, again. Rats!

Quadrant Three: Move

The bodies we travel through this life in are made to move! Our bodies are amazing organisms. We are physiologically designed to do hard physical labor. And to express ourselves! We dance, run, stretch, climb, carry, ride, play, lift, twist, pull, push, and row. We also fight, freeze, and flee. Physical movement is inherent to our survival. Our procreation depends on it. Yet the post-industrial digital information age has made movement all but obsolete. Obesity plagues almost every first-world country. Video games have led to young people feeling more and more alienated from their bodies.

Still, there is hope. Chemicals are released in our bodies during intense physical activity that are inherent not only to optimal performance, but also to our sense of wellbeing.

Neuroscience has led us to understand that the monoamine neurotransmitters – dopamine, serotonin, and noradrenaline – are released during heightened physical activity. In their 2017 book, *Stealing Fire*, Steven Kotler and Jaime Wheal talk about this performance enhancing cocktail, and in his 1990 self-same titled book, Mihaly Csikszentmihalyi identified it as *flow*. Flow is the human brain operating optimally. Kotler and Wheal point out that that these feel-good chemicals so crucial to our brain function act not only as physical performance enhancers; this neuro-cocktail enhances concentration, increases focus, augments reaction time, and magnifies pattern recognition.

For the person with ADHD, this may mean a leveling of the playing field. Intense physical activity can bring dopamine online, enabling the person with ADHD to focus, concentrate, and control impulsivity more effectively. These are the very things stimulant medications such as Adderall and Ritalin hope to achieve, as well.

Quadrant Four: Keep Good Company

For the ADHDer, relationship to others has the same impact as it does on anyone, except that there are times when the ADHDer will need to rely on the executive function (that ability to plan, organize, and manage time) of an other. The ADHD coaching world calls this go-to person the "Body Double." This is an important need to identify because it connects directly with the ADHDer's need for environmental structure and support. It's in these moments of dependence that ADHDers are shamed and blamed because of poor functionality with organizational tasks, timekeeping, and planning. Again, the question is this: would you chastise someone who didn't have legs for not being able to walk? No. You'd probably help them get a wheelchair or prosthetics.

However, I continue to be amazed at the resistance to this idea by people with ADHD, and by their caregivers. ADHDers, who often appear to be functional on so many levels, expect themselves – and are expected by those around them – to function normally. It appears to be very difficult for many to accept the very real limitations that we have. Fortunately, the ADA has recognized ADHD, and therefore, folks with ADHD are afforded accommodation in academic and workplace environments.

KEY POINTS

- Most people with ADHD are time-challenged and loose track of time easily. This can be source of shame and embarrassment.

- Indigenous cultures have a different way of viewing time, one that is more rooted in natural cycle. ADHDers may be better innovators because of their temporal liability.

- Multi-tasking is not possible. ADHDers can appear to be good multi-taskers because they often thrive on the adrenaline response that results from highly stimulating environments. But ADHDers actually struggle with transitions.

- The Time Audit can help the ADHDer identify how we spend our time and what we really care about; what's important to us. Using timekeeping tools is essential to the ongoing functionality of those of us with ADHD.

- The Self Center leads to an understanding of our Internal Commitments. Discipline is being a disciple of our authentic selves.

- The four (4) quadrants of optimal living can help lay the foundation for having a meaningful and fulfilling life. They are Sleep, Eat, Move, and keep Good Relations.

CHAPTER FIVE

Heartfulness

Mindfulness can be useful for everyone, including ADHDers. Mindfulness helps us focus, bringing the attention into the here and now, enabling us to feel calmer. But those of us with ADHD might need a stronger medicine. We might need what I call Heartfulness. While mindfulness meditation helps many, ADHDers tend to have big emotions and have trouble getting okay with them. We can get really blown off track and have a hard time recovering from the upsets that happen in day-to-day life. While Mindfulness deals with the thinking brain, or the growth brain, Heartfulness is designed to deal with the feeling brain, the part of us that gets ramped and revved up to the point of being a problem. Heartfulness combines physical, or what's called somatic movement activities with creative visualization and image-based exercises aimed at cultivating feelings states. In many cases, Mindfulness meditation is just too difficult for ADHDers. We just can't sit still long enough for it to work.

ADHD is not the only condition that has trouble with big emotions. Nervous systems are hard to wrangle. Just the term nervous tells us we might be in tough territory here. The feeling brain, or survival brain is linked directly to the nervous system. A lot of other conditions can look like ADHD, so it's important to rule out other conditions, called disorders by the medical world by consulting with one, if not several qualified medical professionals before determining that you actually have ADHD. The good news is that Heartfulness helps regulate any upset nervous system, ADHD, or not.

What We Feel Others See

What does is mean when someone calls us moody? Broody?
Or giddy? High-strung? Distracted? We are not always aware
of our mood or might not even know what mood is. Most of us
ADHDers have trouble identifying and controlling our big feelings. They take us by surprise. And we are perplexed when others can see how we feel when we can't.

Sometimes we hear people talking about our *affect*. What the
heck does *that* mean? What does it have to do with our feelings
and how we are? Affect deals with how others see us emotion-
ally, while mood is how we experience emotions ourselves. Our
affect might be described as "bright" if we are feeling upbeat and
positive about life. We might be really happy about something,
or just generally feel good. A bright affect means we might be
smiling and attentive, and appear to be in a good mood. Or our
affect can be described as "flat." A flat affect means we are kind
of listless and our voice is monotone, like we don't have a whole
lot invested in what's going on right now, like we've given up.
We might be upset about something or feel despondent, or hopeless. A lot of us with ADHD struggle with mood because of the
challenges we face in environments that aren't good for us, or
with our own brand of the Shame Blame Game.

Anxiety and ADHD

We all feel anxious sometimes, whether we have ADHD or
not. It's important to distinguish anxiety from ADHD. Anxiety
can be feeling upset about an important event. It can be distress
or uneasiness. It can also come from unresolved conflicts, or
things we are afraid of, real or imagined. Anxiety often looks
like ADHD. Anxiety can lead to difficulty in focusing. It can
make it hard to sit still, and it can make us do things without
thinking them through. Anxiety can come from stuff we are
upset about in the past, or it can come from stuff we are facing
right now, such as being really worried about passing a very important test.

Big feelings come from how we were before we could think,
before cognition developed. When we were under eighteen
months old we just sort of absorbed the world around us like a
sponge. How we felt came from a combination of our innate be-

ing, and what was going on around us. If we felt like the world was a safe place we were less afraid, and felt more relaxed. Our wellbeing was supported. But if we experienced the world out there was dangerous, we felt pretty freaked out. These are called *secure and insecure attachment styles,* and can play a key role in how safe we feel in relationships with others.

Later we'll explore how stressors rooted in relationships can trigger ADHD-like symptoms, but may not be ADHD. Securely attached people will most likely find ways of maintaining healthy connections with others. They may be less prone to shame and are able to find healthy ways to process anxiety. Those of us that are anxious-preoccupied ADHDers will be more prone to outbursts and impulsivity. We might have a harder time dealing with our emotions, and blame ourselves, or others for our upsets.

Those of us who are dismissive/avoidant may have a hard time admitting that we have a problem, and it's more likely we may be in denial. We might attempt to hide our feelings, and be defensive if others point our big feelings out.

Fear-avoidant ADHDers may have a hard time trusting others, and may feel anxious in relationships. Anxiety exacerbates ADHD symptoms, making it more difficult to concentrate, sit still, and control impulses. Those of us with a fear-avoidant attachment style may crave closeness but have trouble trusting. This is sometimes part of a cycle, as the fear of being hurt can often make ADHD symptoms worse.

Fear-based thoughts and feelings impact our outlook and can render us frozen in thought and action. This is what characterizes the survival brain. What is the purpose of fear? How does it serve us? How does it hinder? When can anxiety be good? Is it *distress,* or *eustress,* a moderate, beneficial stress? By changing our physiology we not only can change our minds, we can change our feeling state. ADHD medications change the physiology through stimulating the body and mind. But we can do this by practicing Heartfulness, with or without psychiatric medications. Deep breathing, meditation, intense physical exercise, creative visualization, and active imagination can all help alleviate anxiety. Often the best cure for anxiety is action.

Depression and ADHD

Depression has been called "anger turned inward." It has come to be seen as bad, because it can lead to violence. But anger is really just life force attempting to assert itself. We get angry when we feel some important aspect of our lives is being threatened. This anger and frustration can come as the result of not being able to effectively meet the expectations of those around us. If we believe we are unable to change, we may feel defeated and want to give up, which only leads to further feelings of hopelessness and helplessness. This can lead to impulsive angry outbursts, or worse. For some it can seem as if there is no way out from the demoralization we face as the result of living with ADHD.

Women with ADHD are sometimes diagnosed as girls with depression rather than ADHD because they feel so knocked down by trying to cope with the challenge of living with it. We might consider the *source* of the depression. This means that for those of us with ADHD, we need to consider that ADHD itself might be the cause of our depression. Exercises and somatic techniques, such as Peter Levine's *Pronking*, and creative visualization, such as the *Freeze Frame* exercise outlined by the HeartMath Institute can change the emotional experience and provide a ray of hope. Heartful practices can light the way out of the dismal corridors of depression.

Jetsunma Tenzin Palmo, a Buddhist nun, talks about "the practice of loving kindness." She points out that being kind and loving toward people who are kind and loving is easy. She says the true test of practicing loving kindness is to do so when people are behaving horribly. This does not mean allowing others to abuse you. If you are being treated badly or abused, do not tolerate it. However, we can augment our behavior to change our feeling state. We can…

1. Change the proximity between you and the other toward whom you feel angry, resentful, or rageful (in other words remove yourself form the source of the stress)
2. Wait until a time when you are both calm and use "I" statements to tell them how you feel.
3. Tell them you don't want to discuss what's upsetting to you anymore.

At the time that our blood is boiling, we are in a state of emotional dysregulation: we are not in control of ourselves. This is why anger and rage can be so detrimental to those with ADHD. At these times, we are at a higher risk for hurting ourselves and others, so augmenting behavior is crucial to a positive outcome. Since ADHDers are already at a disadvantage due to underdeveloped executive functioning, it is essential that a behavioral plan be put in place to help regulate difficult situations, such as changing proximity to the source of stress until you calm down.

Everyone practices varying degrees of self-regulation. The survival brain controls emotional responses in the face of perceived threat. But for those who have ADHD, the severity of dysregulation can be amplified, leading to extreme behaviors. The combination of a delayed development in the pre-frontal cortex and an overactive amygdala can be deadly. It is important to have systems in place ahead of time to be prepared for when – not if, but when, we become dysregulated. How are we going to manage it? How we you going to keep from raising our voice, from saying things you'll regret, from using profanity, from even becoming physically riled up and throwing things, destroying property or, God forbid, becoming physically violent with another. No one likes to talk about this stuff, but we all know it happens. And it can contribute significantly to the shame spiral that many ADHDers feel when they have outbursts.

During the second Iraq war in 2004, I read an article by a spiritual teacher who remarked on the peace marchers who hit the streets and were reminiscent of the Viet Nam protesters in the 1960s. The writer pointed out that if we want to be peace activists, we need to begin with the violent impulses in our own hearts. I thought about the necessary driving I had to do through the streets of Los Angeles on a regular basis, and I remembered the violent rage that bubbled up in me whenever some A-hole would cut me off. Basically this teacher was suggesting that while she admired the marchers demonstrating for peace, this sort of self-cognizance was the best way to truly be a peace activist.

In order to plan our self-regulation effectively, it's important to work with a coach to determine what specifically gets our blood boiling. From there, you can develop ways to mitigate the effects of dysregulation that are tailor-made for you, and which will actually work in our environment. You may need to collaboratively create a Safety Plan with caregivers, teachers, co-workers, and the people you live with. That may mean working with an ADHD Coach, a Behavioral Analyst, or even a Family Systems Therapist. You will likely need help from someone who can help you identify sources of de-escalation in your specific environment and coach you on how to use them.

Energy Management

Energy management is how we are able to consciously direct our energy. The human organism is an energetic system comprised of multiple complex systems, including an energetic body that is an electromagnetic field. Quantum Physics tells us our energetic fields are connected to all other living things, to the Earth itself, and possibly the entire universe. When we recognize this, we are able to do certain things to regulate this energetic field.

Think of a pressure cooker. When the water heats up it turns to steam, which can cause pressure in the pot, and make it blow up! Ka-Boom! This is what can happen in our energy systems if we don't regulate. But we can do things to regulate our energy systems. In the same way that a speaker can get blown by turning the volume up too loud, or a light bulb gets burned out and can explode by a power surge, too much energy that is not grounded can damage our energetic systems.

This is why physical movement and deep breathing are so crucial to the regulation of the human energetic system. When we run, for example, through physical exertion our hearts beat faster and our lungs draw in more breath. Oxygenating the blood helps produce more feel good chemicals. High intensity physical exercise can expel the distress that can lead to depression.

Developing the executive function of the brain, the *thinking brain* leads to increased volitional consciousness. We are all conscious choice makers. When we are able to control the input and outflow of our own energy, we feel much more in control of ourselves.

Some say that people with ADHD vibrate at a higher rate than other folks. What we do know is that ADHDers can sometimes have moods that swing up and down, where we experience feelings of being able to take on the world followed by feelings of defeat and frustration at not being able to impact the world around us at all. If we have tools and systems in place to deal with these mood fluctuations, we are much more likely to better deal with what's going on.

KEY POINTS

- Heartfulness deals with the issue of emotional regulation. ADHD is not so much a deficit of attention, as it is of the ability to regulate emotions.

- Mood is what we feel and affect is what others see when we feel something. Sometimes we don't see our emotions but others do.

- Anxiety is crippling to the ADHDer. It can exacerbate poor concentration, and increase difficulty sitting still. Heartful practice can help alleviate anxiety.

- Depression can occur as the result of feeling hapless and helpless in the face of ADHD. Heartful practices such as HeartMath Freeze Frame and Peter Levine's Pronking can help us feel less depressed.

- The Heartful practice of Loving Kindness toward people who challenge us can not only lead to our feeling better, but may actually reduce violence in the world.

- Use of the Thinking Brain can be a Heartful practice to override fear and anger impulses associated with the Survival Brain.

CHAPTER SIX

Autopilot

How does autopilot work on a jet airliner? Let's say you're on a jet plane that takes off in Los Angeles and is destined for Paris, France. Let's say you make repeated trips on this flight, but the flight keeps winding up in Hong-Kong. This would lead not only to your insisting you get your money back from such a disreputable airline, but you would probably be frustrated to the point of loosing your cool, a cool you worked so hard to acquire by using the Heartful practices from the previous chapter. Yet, this is an example of just how the unconscious mind works. No matter how many times we tell ourselves that we won't be late, if our unconscious belief is that we will be late, guess what? You got it! We'll be late because that's what we believe deep down about ourselves. Our unconscious beliefs dictate where we go, what we do, and how we do it.

So how do we change our unconscious beliefs? It starts with asking, what do we believe about ourselves? What do we believe about ADHD? Do we believe that because we have ADHD, we are disabled; that we have a disorder? As we explored earlier when we were talking about shame and blame, words are powerful. Words define us. Look, the last "D" in ADHD stands for *disorder*. How many times have we heard, "are you ADHD?" How many times have we heard, "My son's ADHD?" Or, "I'm ADHD," as if we were defined as a *disorder*!

Our beliefs about ourselves are shaped by the words we use to describe ourselves. These beliefs shape what we do. So if we don't really believe we can go from LA to Paris, no matter how many times we tell ourselves otherwise, we will wind up in Hong Kong because that's where we believe we belong. But if we want the plane to go from LA to Paris, and it keeps going to Hong Kong, what do we do? How can we course correct?

Once we have our vision, that is, once we know where we want to go, we need something that's going to move us toward our vision of what we really want. We need to develop something that sets us squarely in the new and preferred version of ourselves that is sustainable in the face of the challenges that will inevitably creep up. We need to reinforce the new Self to remain consistent with the chosen and practiced version of its Self. The unconscious mind needs messages on a consistent basis until it comes to believe that it is possible to attain the desired outcome. That outcome is the desired and preferred version of our Selves. Paris over Hong Kong. No offence to anyone reading this in Hong Kong!

Of course, this is more difficult than it sounds. Establishing any new habit on a consistent basis in order to change our Self-concept is one of the most difficult things a person can attempt. Try it and you'll see what I mean. But don't try it and see what happens. Sometimes, you might be ripe for change and feel ready for it; then, it can come easy. This is often the case with disasters, or major life shifts that are beyond our control. The axiom is, *change or die*. But to *induce* the change can be like chewing razor blades and staring into the abyss. We tend toward the comfortable: comfort foods, alcohol, drugs, sugar, video games, sex, TV, etc. But as productivity coach, Tim Ferris, points out - life begins where comfort ends. The only way out is through. Moving into discomfort really can be the easier, softer way because it inspires growth over stagnation. But it may challenge our fundamental beliefs about ourselves.

Our core beliefs are layer upon layer of thoughts that are infused with emotion. This is how a downward spiral can creep up on us, taking us down like a linebacker tackling a running back on the opposing team who thought the touchdown was guaranteed. Core beliefs are formed before we can think for ourselves and are influenced by our family and our culture. For example, intergenerational trauma has an impact on people living now. The experiences and difficulties that our grandparents and great-grandparents underwent contribute to the beliefs we have now. So what role do our beliefs play in shaping our experience? Mid-twentieth century plastic surgeon, Maxwell Maltz was astonished when his previously disfigured patients, after surgery would continue to see themselves as they were before the surgery. Drawing from Prescott Lesky's Self-Consistency Theory, Dr. Maltz developed his book Psycho-Cybernetics. He introduced the ideas of visualizations and affirmations to a generation of mostly business people who wanted to improve their professional performance and sales.

Dr. Maltz based Psycho-cybernetics on the idea of mechanical cybernetics. For example, a thermostat is a cybernetic mechanism. If it gets too cold, the thermostat turns the heat on. If it gets too warm, it turns it off, keeping the temperature at a steady comfortable level. This is the same principal as the autopilot system in the jet plane. The autopilot is programmed to take being knocked off course as the result of turbulence into consideration. It course corrects automatically. Psycho-Cybernetic is the same kind of mechanism in our unconscious mind. But in order to understand this more clearly we need to look more closely at the relationship between our feelings, thoughts, and what we do.

Tools for Reprograming Unhelpful Beliefs

Long before Sigmund Freud, who is considered the father of modern psychotherapy, a German doctor, Franz Mesmer, identified an unconscious force that he called magnetism. While magnetism, or mesmerism was never embraced by the scientific community because of its inability to be empirically proven, it became the basis of hypnosis, a system that puts people into a heightened state of concentration that makes them more easily influenced by the suggestions of the hypnotist. In a sense the hypnotist is speaking to the unconscious beliefs of the person being hypnotized. Hypnotism has taken on a level of recognition by the field of psychology as a viable tool or intervention in particular for breaking bad habits, such as cigarette smoking and overeating. It has also garnered reported success at overcoming extremely negative emotions.

In the next chapter we will explore cognitive behavioral therapy, a form of therapy that has reported success in treating ADHD.

KEY POINTS

- The unconscious mind is like the autopilot cybernetic mechanism in an airplane that is pre-programed to fly from one location to another. This is referred to as Psycho-Cybernetics by Dr. Maxwell Maltz.

- The unconscious mind dictates what we believe. Words and ideas that we use without being fully aware of them influence how we feel about ourselves.

- Core beliefs are layer-upon-layer thoughts that we may have had without being fully aware of their impact on our feeling state.

- Mesmerism evolved into hypnosis. Hypnosis is regarded as an effective tool for overcoming unwanted habits.

CHAPTER SEVEN

Mindfulness

Mindfulness is a Buddhist concept that has been co-opted by Western psychology and turned into a billion dollar industry. Anglican Priest, noted philosopher and drunkard, Alan Watts, stated back in the 1960s that Eastern philosophy and mysticism would find its roots in Western soil. Yoga certainly is evidence of this. Yoga took off like wildfire in the 1980s and is now a mainstay of Western intersection between physical fitness and spirituality. Mindfulness has joined the ranks of Eastern concepts that have taken root in Western soil and grown into a familiar intervention for achieving not just mental health, but peace-of-mind and fulfillment as well. Translated from Sanskrit, the term *Mindfulness* literally translates as "to recollect, to remember," and "to bear in mind." We ADHDers may see this as collecting our whole Selves, Selves that have been fragmented and disintegrated by distress and the energetic toxicity of shame. We might see this as *re-membering, becoming a member again* of the ADHD Tribe where we can gain acceptance, efficacy, and a sense of well-being and belonging.

I Feel, Therefore I Think, Therefore I Do

A few years back I worked with a college student named Devin. Devin was a scifi fan. Like many living with ADHD, he struggled with the mundane minutia of day-to-day life. He hated the administrative tasks of "the daily grind." But he had an extraordinary super-power of abstract intelligence. He'd learned that imagination is the key to getting the necessary dopamine online for concentration and focus. He knew that a little fun before a hard task would optimize brain chemistry.

When I introduced the idea of *Cognitive-Behavioral Triangles* to

Devin, he yawned, and like cartoon character, he drooped down onto the desk, melting into a drippy, droopy, pile of goo on the floor. I knew we were in trouble!

I resorted to my bag of magical tricks. I knew the *Bag of Yuck*, a bag of slimy, sticky, rubber worms, cockroaches, and rats, would not work because Devin was a college student, and such things would have seemed infantile to him. So I broke out my Bad Assed 3' x 2' sticky notes, plastering them onto his dorm center wall. Then I reached for my markers and drew a triangle.

I put an F at the top, to represent Feelings, because feelings always show up first. I then rooted the base of the triangle with a T and an A. While Devin might have been thinking his own thoughts about T&A, fondly recalling spring break in a totally inappropriate manner for ADHD coaching, I deftly guided his precious attention back to the triangle, stressing the power of T for Thoughts, and A for Action. Lessons on respecting women would come on another day.

Devin sat back for a moment and took in my diagram,. A vibrant discussion about the remake of Battle Star Galactica ensued. BSG for short. Devin and I were both huge BSG fans at the time, and if Devin's parents, who were footing the bill for his coaching – had walked in on us, they might have asked what the hell BSG had to do with ADHD and promptly fired me! But what they might not have understood is that I was helping Devin associate his ideas with something that was not only meaningful to him, but something that had a lot of juice for him. Again, think dopamine.

We talked about the Jump Drive, or Faster Than Light (FTL) hyper-drive, that showed up in a lot of twentieth century sci-fi and was integral to the plot line of BSG. Well, it was as if the right neurotransmitters collided, and Devin's face lit up with what appeared to be an inner glow, the likes of which Abraham Maslow would have been proud. In this enlightened moment, Devin renamed my *Cognitive-Behavioral Triangles* the FTA Drive, referencing the BSG Jump Drive. Only in science fiction can we go faster than light. But with ADHD, it can seem like feelings, thoughts, and actions tear through our world like a storm in Tornado Alley ripping and tearing us asunder.

We began this discussion with the topic of Mindfulness. Cognitive-behavioral triangles are a part of a system called

Cognitive-Behavioral Therapy, or CBT, that works well with ADHD. Since cognition is a function of mind, Buddhists may be seen as the original cognitive-behavioral therapists.

CBT can be found in everyday life. Ideas like *all or nothing thinking,* and *reality testing,* come from CBT. Words like never and always are examples of all or nothing, or *black and white thinking* - extremes that are often used inaccurately, when sometimes might better describe a situation. Testing our perceptions against others can be a way of figuring out if we are seeing things whack-a-do, or if we nailed it. Buddhists talk about *Monkey Mind,* the inner chatter that just rattles on and on with no real basis in reality. Mindfulness is the practice of breaking out of the spell of Monkey Mind to bring our attention back into the present moment.

Devin renamed emotions feelings, cognition, thoughts, and behavior, actions – forming the F-T-A.

Emotions = Feelings
Cognition = Thoughts
Behavior = Action

First we feel things, then we think about them, and finally we do things based on how we feel and what we think. When our cat walks into the room purring, we might feel all warm and tingly. The first thing we are aware of is a feeling. We might think, "Aw, how cute. I'm so happy my cat is purring right now." The feeling state generates a thought. Then we might pet the cat, scratch their belly, and make a funny sound like a cat. That's the thing we do: an action or a behavior. This depicts the FTA Drive. Feeling, thought, action.

Feelings Are Not Facts

Science tells us our feeling state shows up first. Our response to this might be: "No-Duh!" It might seem obvious that we are sponges observing and absorbing our environment. But a feeling state is an amorphous experience that has no ability to label, process, or decide what to do it. For people with ADHD, big feelings or emotions can cause impulsive behavior that gets us in trouble. If we get excited about something, we might leap up, spilling hot coffee all over our new work clothes and burning ourselves in the process. Hopefully, we didn't spill the coffee on our new electron-

ADHD, A HEARTFUL APPROACH

ic notebook, or worse yet, our boss's new electronic workbook. Or even worse yet, on our boss. Yikes! We might find ourselves calling Aunt Tootsie, who we know will talk forever, when we only have a few minutes, then we're surprised when it's impossible to get off the phone with her. Or worse, maybe we left our toddler in the grocery cart as we go tearing out of the parking lot, panicked because we've left the garden hose on at home and it's going to flood our next door neighbor's flower garden – the neighbor who already called the cops on us the last time we forgot our keys and were trying to break into our house, setting off the alarm. Like, really? Didn't she realize my new black beanie and dark grey jogging suit only somewhat resembles a cat burglar's outfit? Ah, ADHD. It's not just a neurophysiological brain condition; it's an adventure and way of life!

I Think, Therefore I...Huh

Then cognition comes on line. Hopefully. Cognition is the ability to think about what is happening. It involves intelligence, learning, memory, language, and a synthesizing of concepts with increasing complexity. Descartes said, "Cogito ergo sum:" I think, therefore, I am. While it might be fun to debate the philosophical tenets of this claim, for the purposes of this work, we'll just say this: thoughts happen! What we do with our thoughts is crucial to all, but with ADHD, the part of the brain that thinks is often delayed or off-line.

Although sensations and feelings show up before cognition, what Descartes might be driving at is that these sentient experiences are meaningless without thinking. Thinking is awareness, awareness is consciousness, and consciousness is identity. Identity tells us who we are in relationship to the world around us. Many of us with what we call ADHD – a label that is held by our cognition – have a certain identity that goes with it. Many people roll their eyes when someone says they have ADHD, but this is because there has been a fair amount of misunderstanding around it. For example, it would be inhumane to roll our eyes at someone who can't walk because they don't have legs, and it would seem ridiculous to tell that same person to "just try harder." They have no legs! Cognition serves us here as a way to understand what ADHD is, and it can be a way to place intellect over emotion when thinking about, navigating, and negotiating our way through the complex maze of unconscious emotions. Cognition gives us a dispassionate view of things – "Just the facts Ma'am!" The facts enable us to become calm and carefully plan our next step.

You Are What You Do

That next step is action. We are defined by what we do, right? Recently in my life, a conflict developed with a close friend over food. I was accused of obsessing and talking endlessly about food. My friend knows that I have a background in fitness and nutrition, and that it's important to me. The criticism made me mad because I felt disrespected, in spite of attempting to convey how important this issue is to me. Finally, I was compared to people who, in my friend's opinion, annoyingly and endlessly post pictures of food on the Internet. By that time my blood was boiling.

Later, in moments of quiet reflection, I had to ask myself why I'd brought such a negative charge to the moment. Why was I so vulnerable to what I experienced as belligerence? This, of course, is the "T" aspect of the FTA: cognition. As it turned out, that moment activated residual emotions from my family of origin that left me feeling diminished, demeaned, and demoralized. These negativistic thoughts, feelings, and action patterns colored my experience of identity when I was too young and underdeveloped to know what was happening. Core beliefs shine out through our emotional experience from the unconscious. And having ADHD itself can be the source of negativistic beliefs.

If we believe that having ADHD makes us a victim of the "disorder," and we then subject ourselves to criticism from people who don't understand ADHD or who might not even believe in it, we have cast ourselves into a victim role by believing that the disorder is insurmountable and that we can't live a full and purposeful life as the result of it. This would be an example of a negativistic core belief. We might even find that this belief is connected to other aspects of our lives as well. We may find ourselves feeling subject to conditions and circumstances beyond our control, believing that fundamentally, the world is not a safe place and that the world around us will hurt or control us.

Or, like me until nearly age 40, you might not even know you have ADHD. You may have been fortunate enough to stumble into circumstances and conditions that have emphasized your strengths, and from there been able to garner resources to engage others to help you with the things you're not good at. You may have done this with grace, poise, and gratitude; you fundamentally believe that the world around you is a safe and benevolent place, that your needs are going to get met no matter what, and that you are likely to have a deeply fulfilling and meaningful life where you are mostly able to meet your goals and experience what you want in life.

What are the fundamental differences here? I often use Donald Trump and Trevor Noah as examples here. Trump grew up with privilege and resources, yet he expresses the belief that fundamentally the world is unsafe and that people are out to get him. Noah grew up in a South African slum, yet he expresses the belief that fundamentally the world is a safe and benevolent place; he therefore treats others with kindness and generosity. So, clearly our life circumstances do not have to dictate our outlook, disposition, and attitude toward ourselves in relationship to the world around us. What does then? And more importantly, if we are not happy with our outlook, attitude, and disposition, can we change it?

Using cognitive triangles, we are able to obtain a more realistic view of ourselves in our relationship with the world around us. Using thoughts, we can change our perception, thereby changing our perspective of ourselves to a more human and Heartful one. We can incorporate intuition, balance, poise, and flexibility by changing our focus from the head to the heart.

But, if you're anything like me, you could be thinking, *Yeah, right! I'm going to think my way into feeling better?* No, it's not that simple. Some of you reading this may remember the Saturday Night Live character, Stuart Smalley, who in the early 1990s mocked the self-help movement and made affirmations totally uncool. Well, I'm here to tell you: he was wrong! Affirmations are one of the keys to turning negative self-concepts and feelings into positive ones.

The other key is Contrary Action, or doing the opposite of what you feel like doing; for example, *not* punching out the a-hole who's trashing your favorite sports team, political candidate, or favorite auntie.

Remember, willpower is limited, so here's where Psycho-Cybernetics meets cognitive-behavioral triangles. Through daily practice of combining Contrary Action with the FTA drive, we can establish new thought-and-action based patterns that will ultimately – after practicing for ten to sixty days – alter our core beliefs in significant ways. Think of it as sending in a construction crew to work on Goof-Ball Island from the Pixar film, *Inside Out*.

It's possible that our core beliefs may require a major over-haul, and it takes time to get a total makeover. Time, repetition, and practice. Here's where willpower is our friend. Initially, it can be like pushing the merry-go-round, but ultimately, a body in motion stays in motion. Once we get our new core beliefs up and running, they take on a gravity of their own.

Making Believe

Beliefs are powerful. Beliefs can be dangerous. But our beliefs can also be the basis of making our dreams come true. They can be our best friends or our worst enemies. In his book, *Free Will*, secular humanist, Sam Harris discusses the dangers of beliefs. He points out that beliefs have often been at the root of violent crimes. He discusses the power of beliefs that are held in spite of evidence to the contrary, and speculates about the origin of beliefs being familial and cultural.

How can it be that, even when confronted with evidence to the contrary, people continue to believe what they have previous-ly been oriented toward? The Internet has given higher visibility to some of our more outlandish beliefs; there are people who be-lieve that the earth is flat, and people who believe that the moon landing was faked in a Hollywood studio. While these beliefs may seem absurd to the most reasonable among us, the polarizing 2016 US presidential election has driven tightly held beliefs to the surface, so that many, upon encountering them, are driven to hys-terics in terms of both laughter and fury. It is probably safe to say that our beliefs shape the world in which we live. And people are still put to death for their beliefs. So this is serious business.

Meanwhile, ADHD remains a controversial topic in many corners of the scientific, medical, and mental health worlds. In spite of recent evidence that ADHD is a neurophysiological devel-opmental brain condition, some people still question its validity and existence. The fact that ADHD symptoms look like so many other conditions is part of the confusion and misinformation. It continues to be misdiagnosed, both when the condition is there, and when it is not. In the early twentieth century what Sir George F. Stills framed as a moral issue became ADHD. It was then called minimal brain dysfunction. ADHD did not exist in its current form until 1968. Since then it has been misunderstood and misappropriated. It would seem that a generation of physicians have prescribed stimulant medications to children and college students who, responding to impossibly competitive academic conditions, used the stimulant medications to get a leg up in their academic careers. This has contributed to the confusion and controversy around what it is. According to Alan Schwartz in his book *ADHD Nation*, ADHD would appear to be a mental illness largely manufactured by scientists and doctors who were on the take from the very pharmaceutical companies that manufacture the stimulant meds they are prescribing. Schwartz points out that leading voices in the ADHD field are actually paid spokespeople for the stimulant meds.

Unlike conduct disorder or personality disorders characterized by a lack of empathy, including other neurophysiological brain conditions, ADHD is characterized not by a lack of empathy but by other behaviors that do not at all reflect on a person's ability to perform moral reasoning. Yet is has been strongly associated with behaviors that could be seen as immoral. ADHD remains in the diagnostic manuals a largely behavioral issue.

Rethinking Positive Thinking

Above is the title of a book by Dr. Gabriele Oettingen that highlights the failure of conventional positive thinking. Dr. Oettingen points out that positive thinking is helpful when we want to sketch out the possibilities for our future, but that it needs to be combined with thinking through the realities that we all face. From this perspective, she developed the WOOP formula:

W – is for wish.
O – is for outcome
O – is for obstacle
P – is for plan – (if this, then that)

Thinking May Save the World

To say that the FTA Drive can save the world may be a bit dramatic! But as the late great sage Carl Sagan pointed out, if we are to survive the next hundred years, it will be the result of applying reason over emotion. Dr. Sagan pointed out that humanity is on the brink of many exciting discoveries, but that our old survival brain hardware may well be our demise. The part of the brain that mitigates the fight, flight, freeze mechanism (FFF) is the old part of the brain needed for survival. Humans have historically been warring tribal animals, yet, today, it's easy to forget that we are animals – mammals to be specific – and that we survived for thousands of years using the autonomic nervous system's FFF response, a reliable mechanism that would alert us to danger. It was eat or be eaten. When a tiger chased us, we either fought, hoping to kill it, ran from it, or played dead, hoping it would lose interest in dead meat. The FFF response kept us safe and alive. But as we have progressed into a global village, with well over seven billion inhabitants, this old brain hardware does not serve us in the way it used to. Science points out that the FFF response mechanism cannot differentiate between a real or perceived threat. Our underlying belief in an external threat remains the source of war, even when there's evidence to the contrary. Unreasonable fear keeps the FFF mechanism over stimulated, keeping the thinking brain muted.

Motivation and Willpower – Why-Flyin'

Another way of framing Contrary Action is "Why Flyin," or WYFLION. WYFLION stands for:

W- Whether
Y – You
F – Feel
L – Like
I – It
O – Or
N – Not

In a moment of inspiration we may *feel* motivated to change for the better. We may be inspired by some YouTube video, podcast, book, or speech that uplifts our heart and makes us feel like we can take on the world! We are invincible! Our super powers are guaranteed and are woven securely into our fabric. Our Invincibility Cloak is working overtime! For Harry Potter fans, that's *invincibility*, not invisibility. But inevitably that luster wears thin. The excitement fades and we are apt to return to what's safe, familiar, and comfortable. It's at that point that the new idea becomes the enemy.

When we do something new that takes us out of our comfort zone it's as if every ounce of inner resistance screams out – "No! No! Don't do it!" Suddenly there is a Greek Chorus inside our heads that seductively coos, "You don't need to go to gym today. Have some more ice cream. You don't need to study for that exam. Just go to bed earlier tomorrow. Eat, drink, stay up late and watch Netflix, for tomorrow will be dreary…" It's as if every dark corner of our Psyche shows up to object to any kind of constructive change. Why is that?

Establishing new habits is the key. Willpower only lasts so long. It's like a battery with a short shelf life. So many things can impact your willpower, such as how much sleep you got last night and how much stress you are under today. Setting new habits requires some will power in the beginning. But once a new and preferred habit is put in place it runs on autopilot, as a psycho-cybernetic flow. So regardless of how you feel, you will likely continue in the preferred habit.

Tools for Grounding

Some simple examples of grounding activities are: doing the dishes, listening to music, going for a walk, brewing a cup of tea, taking a cold shower, taking a hot bath, or talking to a friend. Having cues in our environment, including supportive relationships, is the key to changing what we do. Contrary action means acting our way into a different feeling state which then results in positive and affirming thoughts, not the other way around. Action is the key. Changing our behavior is the key to changing our lives and changing the world. When we are calm and in full command of our cognitive function, we are in a much better state to effectively address conflict. Developing cognitive function is the key to increased overall functionality for the person with ADHD. It is also the key to effective solution identification, solutions that are win-win for all involved. This is how we change the world. You can save the world by changing the FTA Drive to the AFT Drive.

KEY POINTS

- Mindfulness is a Buddhist concept that translated from Sanskrit means "to bear in mind."

- The cognitive triangle is part of a system called Cognitive Behavioral Therapy, or CBT that places an emphasis of thought over emotion. We lead with the feeling state, but can change our feeling state though actions and thoughts.

- CBT activates the Thinking Mind and challenges Monkey Mind and *all or nothing thinking* influenced by fear and the Survival Mind.

- We are defined by our actions, not our thoughts or feelings.

- WOOP is a system designed to "rethink positive thinking." WOOP stands for Wish, Obstacle, Outcome, Plan - and is a system devised to help us overcome obstacles and meet our goals.

- Why Flyin', or WYFLION stands for *whether you feel like it or not* and represents the idea of Contrary Action, a concept wherein we do the opposite of what we feel like doing because we know it's good for us or is the right thing to do.

CHAPTER EIGHT

Context is Everything!

The Reasonable Man adapts himself to the world: the unreasonable one persists in trying to adapt the world to himself. Therefore, all progress depends on the unreasonable man. —G. B. Shaw

I was lucky enough to spend the majority of my youth in work situations that highlighted my strengths. By day I cleaned houses, by night I sang in a rock band. The vainglory of rock stardom included schlepping everyone else's equipment because, when you're the singer, you only have to lug around a microphone, so you become a helping pair of hands for the other band members. Our evenings were spent rehearsing for 3-5 hours a night, 3-5 nights per week, losing my voice in rehearsal, paying a lot for the rehearsal space, schlepping equipment to and from rehearsal, and gigging until 4 o'clock in the morning. But hey! I loved my job, and I loved the other guys in the band. I was the old man at age 21. The drummer, bass player, and guitarist were all still in high school. I rented a room in a boarding house. By day, I supported myself by scrubbing toilets, vacuuming and waxing floors, and endlessly dusting my way through suburban New Jersey. By night I was a Rock God, the lead singer for a band called Bittersweet! (Yes, you can YouTube it. Just type in my name and Bittersweet.) Gigging until 4:00am didn't make for terrific 8:00am house cleaning appointments, but bleary eyed, with coffee in one hand and dust rag in the other hand, I'd get to it.

It sounds worse than it actually was. Truth is, I enjoyed being left alone with my thoughts during the day, and cleaning houses made me feel like I was actually accomplishing something because cleaning is one of those things that, when you do it, you see immediate tangible results, which can be quite gratifying. I didn't know I had ADHD at the time, but I was able to be constantly on the move, keep my own schedule, and totally control my environment. For the most part, my clients were not at home, so I would go into a cleaning frenzy then kick back and imbibe caffeine and sugar, watching a little MTV before getting back to business.

After Bittersweet's failed attempt at a contract with CBS records in 1987, CBS records was sold to SONY, and any hopes of making it big as a Rock Star dried up. As a complete non sequitur, I left my band to try my hand as a fitness trainer. Second to being a front man for a rock band, my biggest passion was working out. Like cleaning houses, fitness required non-stop movement. And who doesn't want to live in a gym? So I marched off to New York City and bought a gym, where I literally lived in the front office, a 6' x 10' cinder blocked space. Good times!

I guess scrubbing grimy bathtubs was not enough to dispel my frenetic energy. I couldn't wait to get to the gym and start to lift weights in hopes of transforming my scrawny-assed physique into something I'd seen in magazines. Amazingly, I actually did that, and then I was put in magazines! I started fitness modeling in 1994, about seven years after starting to work out. Did I mention that I smoked cigarettes? Yeah. A lot. I smoked a pack and a half a day.

Looking back now, knowing what I do about ADHD, I can see that the stimulants of caffeine and nicotine helped calm me and keep me focused. I used to joke that cardiovascular aerobic exercise helped distribute the nicotine to all the vital organs. It was easy to drop down to 5 or 6% body fat for a photo shoot on a steady diet of cigarettes and coffee. It made me feel like I didn't want to eat. I had to force myself to ingest egg whites, protein powder, canned tuna, brown rice and broccoli – which is pretty much what I lived on at the time. And I got pretty sick after doing this for a while. Anyone who's told you that fitness has anything to do with health doesn't know the fitness world. None of it would have been possible were it not for the constant addiction to stimulants. I never moved to harder stuff, like crystal meth, because I was already a recovering addict and sober. But I can certainly see why ADHDers are prone to stimulant addiction.

I had no idea at the time that my education in exercise physiology would lead me to an important axiom that would inform my basic understanding of how to live with, and function optimally with, ADHD. Exercise physiology has its roots in basic biology, exploring how food is broken down and used as energy in the body to achieve optimal adaptation, strength, and endurance, enabling the organism – the body – to function optimally. It was here that I learned *physiological adaptation to environmental stimuli*.

What does that mean, you ask?

It means that the world around us shapes us. This is true whether you are a turnip or an artichoke. It's also true whether you are an aardvark or a vermilingua, otherwise known as an anteater. Both creatures have long snouts enabling them to get into tight spots in order to find tasty ants to chow down on. Whether turnip or artichoke, aardvark or anteater, surviving the conditions on this planet has shaped all the life forms on it. You can see this idea explored well on videos that speculate about life on other planets. Gravity, proximity to a host star, water, and magnetic fields all give rise to creating the conditions that enable life on Earth to exist. That is to say that we really are products of the environment. But clearly, once established, we then influence the environment as part of it.

So, what does that mean for ADHD?

ADHD is a relational condition.

I will say it again. ADHD is a relational condition.

ADHD is rooted in the brain. It is innate and inherent to the organism. ADHD symptoms, such as they are described in the ICD-10 and DSM-V, are rooted in the relationship between the brain and the environmental. Therefore, changing environmental conditions can make worse, exacerbate, reduce, or eliminate ADHD symptoms.

Light

In her groundbreaking book, *The Irlen Revolution*, Helen Irlen talks about a perceptual processing problem that, according to her website, impacts about one out of three people with ADHD. She also points out that many, who have been diagnosed with ADHD, dyslexia, and other childhood learning disorders, may have a condition called *Scotopic Sensitivity Syndrome*, or *Irlen Syndrome*. With a research background, Irlen set about trying to figure out why otherwise bright children and adults were struggling with reading. Because difficulty focusing is inherent to ADHD, Irlen Syndrome can look a lot like ADHD. She discovered that a colored overlay over the printed page would make words and charts stop swimming, or pulsing, which is how many who have this condition, including me describe their experience of words and characters on the page. Irlen points out that when the background color is changed behind the characters on the page, it normalizes the brain's ability to process visual information.

When I went to The Irlen Institute in Lakewood, California, I was fortunate enough to be tested by Ms. Irlen herself. I had failed my state boards for the psychotherapist license and was feeling pretty demoralized when a colleague at the community mental health agency I worked for suggested I look into the Irlen Institute. What I discovered astounded me. When she ran the test with me, we discovered that my sensitivity to florescent lighting registered an anxiety response on par with Post Traumatic Stress Disorder. Ms. Irlen told me I had one of the worst cases of Scotopic Syndrome she had ever seen! When she turned on the florescent lighting in the room, which had shades drawn and was dimly lit, I literally flinched and winced. We both laughed. I left with an overlay to use when reading books. The overlay worked on computer screens as well. I promptly wrote to the accommodation office at my licensing board and acquired permission to use the overlay for my exams. It was granted, and I then passed my Marriage and Family Therapist licensing exams.

Sound

In yet another groundbreaking book, *The Highly Sensitive Person*, Dr. Elaine Aron points out that a condition my mother used to call "audio dyslexia" (not an official scientific term!) is actually Sensory Processing Sensitivity, or SPS, or HSP. In the 1990s, Dr. Aron and her husband, Arthur, established a basis for understanding that 15-20% of the population process stimuli "more deeply." According to the Drs. Aron, HSPs are often more aware of subtleties in the environment, are overly sensitive to other's moods, may be overwhelmed by bright lights and loud sounds, startle easily, have difficulty when asked to do too many things at once, try hard to avoid making mistakes or forget things, find changes in their lives are more difficult to adjust to than others, and, after a busy day, may need to withdraw into a darkened room for relief in seclusion.

Many of these characteristics are similar to trauma responses and may or may not be indicative of ADHD. But I propose that many ADHDers are HSPs, and that the "symptoms" of the conditions may be related. More research is needed. But what we do know is that through making changes in the environment, many ADHD symptoms can be greatly reduced. We know that although ADHD is an inherent physiological brain condition, the distress it causes can be ameliorated or reduced by making environmental adjustments. Like Irlen Syndrome, SPS likely concerns various filters in the brain that lead to processing audio-visual information differently. It's likely that filters, which normally filter out stimulation to the brain and central nervous system, are absent in HSPs and those with Irlen Syndrome and ADHD.

Emotional Stress

Distress and anxiety are crippling to the ADHDer. When I worked at the community mental health agency, my coworkers found my constant playing of soothing music on my iPhone amusing. When asked about it, I'd laugh and point out that playing relaxing music helps with my energy regulation. Since ADHD means trouble with emotional regulation, relaxation exercises, physical exercise, meditation, and focusing exercises can be beneficial.

Stress can come from both internal and external sources. When something happens during the day that makes me feel like my reputation or good standing in the community is threatened, or if my financial wellbeing is perceived to be at stake, I have moments of extreme doubt and fear and spiral down into a dark place very quickly. This can be debilitating. In the past, it led to extreme depression that lasted for weeks, or sometimes even months. Although this might happen to anyone with these circumstances, I maintain that the effect is amplified in part because of the innate shame and negativistic narrative discussed earlier that impacts most of us with ADHD.

In Chapter Two we discussed the shame ADHDers feel for their condition, and the blame foisted on them by others, or that we place upon ourselves– what I call a case of the BADS! In general ADHDers have felt bad for their inability to function normally over a prolonged period of time and have internalized very negativistic beliefs about themselves. These negative beliefs can be the cause of extreme distress; ADHDers can over-react to life events where there is a perceived threat. Thus, it doesn't hurt to have an arsenal of regulating techniques and tools at the ready, and at the quick. This Heartful approach is designed to build those tools. What we have learned is that, regardless of the cause, whether it is innate or environmentally induced, if the sympathetic nervous systems is over-active, we need to intercede to help reduce the over-arousal of the nervous system and manage stress. We might see this as stopping to deliberately install an imaginary traffic cop in the pre-frontal cortex that consciously directs, inciting executive function in the brain. This can be done through practice.

Understanding the ADHDer in their environment is crucial to treatment. Whether the stressor is internal or external, the response is always internal and dysregulating. But how we handle it is external, and within our control. So figuring out what works for you or your loved one to help them calm down is key. It can be different for different folks, but the soothing activity should be a healthy one, and one that can be done in the environment around you. There are all kinds of unhealthy activities that can reduce tension, and these include imbibing: too much alcohol; too much Netflix, Hulu, and Amazon Prime; too many video games; too much sugar; and too much sex. The key component here is balance. All of these substances and activities, and the neurochemicals that they stimulate, regulate us in one way or other, but we might be wise to develop response habits, such as the use of relaxing music to help us cope with difficult or unpleasant stress. For folks without ADHD these things are challenging. For those of us with ADHD, distress can be debilitating.

Relational Environment

Looking at our relationships is crucial for the ADHDer. We are organisms in relationships with the world around us. People, animals, and plants are all a part of that. We talked about light, sound, and emotional stress. This can all play into our living and work environments. Is where we live or work noisy? Quiet? What works for you? There are really no two ADHDers that are alike. What kind of relationships do we have with our neighbors? Roommates? Family? Co-workers, bosses, employees? Our dogs, cats, fish, lizards, cacti, or philodendron? People, places, and things play an essential role to feeling good about who we are, what we're doing, and how we are.

Finding relationships that enhance rather than diminish or demoralize can be the difference between someone living the Shame Blame Game or living their Superpowers. Obviously if you are good with numbers and not with people you should not be in sales, but rather in the accounting department. Most of us are better with people than numbers, so we are good in fast paced, hectic environments where our strengths are emphasized. But too much stress might have the opposite effect and demoralize us. So pay attention to *how* you are in the environment that you are in. How do you feel when you're there? How about when you leave?

The same principal can be applied to our relationships with people. I have had supervisors and co-workers who were extremely challenging and difficult to get along with. A little of this is good, as it helps us grow, but working with or for someone who fundamentally doesn't get you can be devastating.

The same is true for dating. If we date or are intimate with accepting and supportive people, not shaming us for forgetting this or that, being late again, or getting upset with us when our attention drifts, we do well. But these traits can be really difficult for our partners and coworkers. It might behoove us to up our game in terms of remembering what these relationships mean to us and using the tools outlined in this book to show our partners we mean business in terms of getting a handle on our ADHD.

It's helpful to pay attention to our environment and how we feel in relationship to it. This includes how we feel in the context of our relationships to the people in our lives. I've worked with kids who were failing one class and getting an A in another. Invariably it's because they feel the teacher who is failing them doesn't like them, and they have a good relationship with the teacher of the class that they get the A in. We are relational learners and excel in environments that are supportive. Conversely we do poorly in environments that are antagonistic. While this may be true for everyone, for those of us with ADHD it can make the difference between failing or getting an A in school, or getting fired from a job, or getting promoted. Being in an environment that works for us can be the single most important thing in terms of a meaningful and fulfilling life. So cultivate those Superpowers and find environments and relationships in which they are celebrated!

Food, Fitness and Finance

What do food, fitness, and finance have to do with each other? And what do they have to do with ADHD?

Food, fitness, and finance are all aspects of how we relate with the world around us. Our habits with each of these can determine the quality of our experience. Each can be connected with grounding activities that warrant less anxiety and increased focus. A healthy eating plan, an effective workout program, and a clear idea of how much money we have, can all lead to a greater sense of wellbeing. If we don't know what we're doing or where we are, we are disoriented, and apt to feel pretty freaked-out. Having a solid plan with food, fitness and money – both how it's earned and how it's managed, can have a profoundly grounding effect on those of us with ADHD.

Some people with ADHD report that eating less refined sugar helps with concentration. Techniques such as *intermittent fasting* also help with focus. Food is Mood. Blood sugar fluctuations can cause severe ups and downs with mood and energy. Mood impacts focus. It's hard to focus when we feel sluggish due to a blood sugar drop. Some nutritional experts recommend that the people with ADHD might well follow a similar eating plan to folks who are hypo-glycemic. This entails eating every two hours, and consuming 20 grams of protein at each meal. Eating this way helps to stabilize blood sugar.

We've previously discussed the impact of high intensity physical exercise and the effect this has on the nervous system and brain. Intense physical exercise stimulates the endocrine system, releasing the stress hormone, cortisol. This stimulates the adrenals thereby releasing feel good chemicals, such as dopamine, leading to more focus. This is the same principal that stimulant meds work on. The methylphenidate, and amphetamine found in most stimulant medications used to treat ADHD, such as Ritalin, Adderall and Concerta keep dopamine hanging out longer, increasing focus.

So what's cash got to do with it? Money is a symbol of value. We determined our values back in the section on the Self-Center, using the Values Compass. How we spend our time tells us about our values. Money is a just a symbol of that. But being clear about matching income with what's needed to support us is grounding. If you are an under-earner – as many with ADHD are – I refer you to Jen Sincero's *You Are A Badass at Making Money*. While she ad-

80

dresses making money, for managing it, I refer you to *Total Money Makeover* by Dave Ramsey. His notion of the *Murphy Fund* is great fun! He stresses the importance of a savings plan, pointing out in a common-sense manner, that it can be the difference between finding ourselves hopeless and homeless, and having a solid ground to stand on – at least financially – which again, leads to feeling safer, more in control, and less anxious. Since anxiety can be crippling to us ADHDers, a solid savings plan is a prescription for calm and focus. This is literally Executive Function.

My Lived Experience

I struggled while working as a therapist in community mental health. The agencies I worked for provide mental heath and developmental supports to people who have mental health conditions, including ADHD. I advocated for the youth and families I worked with. But the environment I had to work in was not conducive to functioning with ADHD. When I advocated for myself, administration seemed more interested in my "productivity" than in the quality of my work. The emphasis was on the documentation of my work, not the quality of the actual work.

I was a good therapist. My strengths are building rapport, establishing authentic relationships, providing empathy, structure, and scaffolding for positive change. Much of my work was successful. But the emphasis in these agencies is documenting in a manner that prevents the insurance companies from taking money back. This creates a fear-based, anxiety-driven, toxic work environment. Charts are often audited and literally millions of dollars are taken back by the government-funded medical insurance, Medi-Cal. Without going too far down the rabbit hole of criticizing the medical field and how it operates, the point is that I was subject to disciplinary action for how I was documenting my work. Legalese and accounting were not my strengths. I really needed the job, but this was not the right context for me. I was "written up," and subject to what is called a "corrective action plan." For someone who took pride in his work, and was actually good at it, this was humiliating and demoralizing. I now had a first-hand experience with how the kids I worked with, who have ADHD, felt in the classroom. Later, when I worked as a supervisor, I was forced to write a therapist up for the same reason. This experience was so disheartening to me that it led to my decision to never work for this kind of agency again.

It was out of the depths of this feeling of demoralization that I forged my own unique way toward understanding what it was that I needed in order to survive, and function in that environment. I carved out a workspace in an office that no one was using and camped out there for several months before I was discovered by the administration and eighty-sixed. (Fortunately, I didn't get written up for that!) By that time I was already working on an upwardly mobile plan to get myself into an environment that was more conducive to my strengths.

Toward the end of my time at that agency, an impromptu concert occurred, involving a harp and a woman who sang like an angel. People poured into the office I was squatting in to see what was going on; even though it wasn't really my office, no one knew any better. Because of having strengths in the area of valuing music, relationships, community, and the ability to appreciate spontaneity, I was able to facilitate and host this Heartful event. This is an example of the kind of creative resilience that we ADHDers have that enables us to rise up and overcome the BIRDSS (barriers, interruptions, re-routing, distractions, snafus, and setbacks) that befall us.

So, if ADHD is for the BIRDSS, we find ways to straighten up and fly right that might not exactly be conventional. We are often told that we need to adapt to the environment. However, what I found is that, to some extent, I needed to adapt the environment to me. In my co-opted office, I was able to beat a hasty retreat from the bright florescent lights and the constant interruptions in the bullpen, a space of adjacent cubicles where everyone gathered as if it were a non-stop party. I needed to get stuff done. I needed to find a way to take care of myself and change the environment to meet my needs, so I could complete my work. For me, soft lighting, soft music in my headphones, a lit candle, some sandalwood incense, and an inspirational figurine instilled my sweet spot environmental formula. Some folks I've worked with have found that by augmenting their environments, they were able to "get *ish* done," as one of my fifteen- year-old clients with ADHD used to say to avoid using profanity.

Tools and Takeaways

Here are some environmentally augmenting and behavioral productivity hacks that might work for folks with ADHD:

- Dimmer lights
- Coffee shop din
- Working at home
- Working remotely
- Working in study groups
- Side barring (engaging in an activity such as doodling)
- Blocking out all social media
- Twirling a basketball
- Using talk to text software
- Having a study buddy
- Non-shaming accountability coach
- Having only one thing on their desk

KEY POINTS

- Our relationship to the world around us shapes who we are, how we develop, and can make the difference between being happy and fulfilled, or being miserable. Change the environment, not the ADHDer. The ADHDer in a better context can greatly reduce ADHD symptoms.

- Irlen Syndrome, or Scotopic Syndrome explores the effects of light in the nervous system. Many people with ADHD have Iren Syndrome. The effects of light with Irlen Syndrom can be as profound as PTSD.

- HSPs or Highly Sensitive People have sensory defensively not just with light, but with sound as well. This condition can look like ADHD and should be considered when ruling ADHD out and treating the symptoms of ADHD.

- Emotional distress from the environment can have an extremely debilitating impact on the ADHDer. Heartfulness can have a positive impact on reducing distress.

- Grounding practices around a food plan, a fitness plan, and good financial management can greatly reduce the anxiety of being disoriented and lost in one's life. ADHDers need grounding.

CHAPTER NINE

Play it Again, Sam!

If you fall, get up. If you fall again, get up again. The journey of
a thousand miles begins with the first step. —LaoZu

Fragile Confidence

No one is perfect.

If you are anything like me, you occasionally forget this.
When we make mistakes, we're often pretty hard on ourselves.
If that's the case, step away from the whip. Acknowledge the
mistake, but let yourself off the hook. Put the weight of the world
down. Relax and live the full catastrophe. Let go and let mess.
Realize and get comfortable with the fact that life is messy. Sit in
the mess. Bask in it. Face it with radical acceptance. Just accept
that there will be times when you will fail miserably and other
people will be upset with you. And you will be upset with others, for what may seem like a good reason, or for no good reason
at all. It's unavoidable. Just own it. It may be a difficult idea to
engage, but try just loving the victim within you. Hold the little
boy or little girl who feels he or she has been wronged by circumstances beyond their control. Don't rely on *fragile confidence*.
Relax and open up to the discomfort of it, and realize that real
confidence is based on Contrary Action, and being in action, even
when you don't feel like it. Always when you don't feel like it.

All of the above is easier said than done. Look, it's not about
avoiding responsibility. And it's normal to feel bad when we
mess up. But for ADHDers, feeling bad can be a way of life. We
need to be careful. Don't over-do the shame and guilt. As we
discussed in Chapter Two concerning the Shame Blame Game,

we can't let those bad feelings keep us from getting up, dusting ourselves off, and getting back into whatever it is that makes us feel groovy and awesome. Just because the imperfections of life interrupt our flow, doesn't mean we can't get back into our flow: flow on, and like Stella, get our groove back! We need to do this over and over, every time.

We live in a world of contradictions. No one is perfect, yet we are all perfect – like the sky. Are trees perfect? Mountains? Clouds? How is it that we seem to be able to appreciate the beauty of nature without negativistic judgments? All right, well, maybe some of you judge nature negatively. But reality is what it is, and we can hold on to our ideas of how we think things should be until the cows come home. But it won't change when they come home. Wait! Where have the cows been? Maybe if we figure out where the cows have been all day, we can figure out the secret to allowing ourselves to be. The cows just wander and graze. They are nature too. And so are we!

More Lived Experience

Some of the obstacles I struggle with are: foggy brain; a feeling I describe as swimming through cement; not getting this book written; feeling scattered; not being able to get my environment organized; getting thrown off course by this breaking or that spilling; or that phone call interrupting my flow. Sometimes, just attempting to do the most mundane tasks can seem insurmountable. I start out thinking, *Oh, this'll just take two seconds.* Then, two hours later….!

Concentrating and staying focused can be quite challenging even when you don't have ADHD. For those with ADHD, it's tough under the best of circumstances. And we all know that circumstances are rarely at their best. Chasing our attention can sometimes feel like chasing a flock of chickens around when they're on amphetamines! At times it may seem that, no matter how hard we try to stay on task, the entire universe has conspired to make it impossible. What can we do, to perform an about-face and face the un-faceable? How can we take our perfectly imperfect selves and make them the BadAsses that Jen Sincero says we can be? How can we live our dreams, whether that means being with the ones you love or loving the ones you're with?

Radical Acceptance

We all know The Serenity Prayer:

Grant me the serenity to accept the things I cannot change
The courage to change the things that I can
And the wisdom to know the difference.

The serenity prayer focuses as much on acceptance as it does on change. What does it mean, to want for nothing? Can we be perfectly happy with our lot in life? We're constantly sent messages that tell us it's not possible; we're told that more is better, that bigger is better. And in some cases that may be true. But in many it is not. It just depends. Circumstances may be different, unique, nuanced, and one-of-a-kind. Generally, quality trumps quantity, and the quality of this experience, right here right now, is really all we have. So, at the heart of the matter, we must consider the things that have an influence on us. These influences can either contribute to or take away from what I call experiential affluence. So maybe Goldilocks had it right. Not too hot, not too cold, not too small, not too big. Just right! In this way, recognizing that there are times when we are foolish, vain, envious, and stubborn is just part of the mix. It's just the deal. How we proceed with this and process it is the thing. If we are able to recognize when and where we are off base, then we have the essence of radical acceptance, which of course, always strives for doing better. We can draw a bigger and bigger circle of acceptance until is encompasses everything in our world.

Change

The other part of the serenity prayer is *changing the things we can*. Recently, I hired a life coach for the first time ever. I had been reading a number of books on coaching that said if you want to be a coach, hire a coach. So I did. In the first session with him, we dove right into the idea of tolerating discomfort. I realized right away that this was not going to be a touchy-feely kind of relationship. Not that he was insensitive – quite the opposite. But he told me up front that there would come a point where I would want a divorce. He told me I would likely wonder what in the Sam Hill I had spent all this money on! And I need to tell you it was a scary amount of money. Sure, I have hired psychotherapists. Even

Jungian Analysts. I have hired massage therapists and personal trainers. But I have never plunked down what felt like it was an inordinate amount of money for eight sessions of unknown adventures with a life coach. Other than graduate school, I had never invested that kind of money in my development before.

Part of my rationale for investing in my growth with a coach was to send myself a powerful message that I am serious about this. I mean business! I really aim to work on myself here. I had to make myself believe that I was committed to making serious change to my current circumstances; I needed to make believe that this change was possible. I needed to establish the frame, or the *temenos*, a Greek term meaning the container in which the alchemical process of transformation can occur. I had to make believe in real change. Making believe is visualizing the results we want and seeing how we will maneuver them. In the case of ADHD, how will we navigate and negotiate the stressors of the day? And we need to practice this over and over, again and again. So, play it again Sam, Miguel, Ashley, Javier, Jamila, Josh, DeMon, Jessica, Devon, Riley, Patty, Chris! Play it again, and again, and again. Our persistence, tenacity, and determination will pay off. I promise!

KEY POINTS

- Fragile confidence is a form of fruitless perfectionism. Get comfortable with the messiness of life.

- Radical acceptance means accepting the things we can't change. The Serenity Prayer offers wisdom and words to live by. That which we resist persists, but when we turn and accept our limitation, the paradox is that this is the path to Heartful peace.

- Changing the things that we can is an important part of feeling empowered. We need to find ways to effect change that we want.

- Making believe – it is often through repetition, practicing something over and over that we get better at it. Investing in our change is crucial. We need to send a message to ourselves that we mean business.

CHAPTER TEN

From Hateful to Heartful!

What does living Heartfully with ADHD look like? What does it mean to live from our Superpowers? Look, while we might not feel on top of things all the time, the hope is that we can shift our baseline from a state of feeling totally demoralized to one of feeling okay at worst, and super stoked at best. It's my sincere hope that this book sheds light on blocks that may have prevented you from feeling good about yourself, and that it has provided you with effective tools to help you get where you want to go. My aim is to tackle the things that prevent us from living up to our full potential. My hope is that by providing tools to help navigate what happens when things get tense, we'll live more solidly in our sense of purpose. Our lives will be more meaningful. We will feel more connected to who we really are, and more significantly connected to those around us.

While it's perfectly normal to feel like crap sometimes, it's not cool to feel that way all the time. This book is meant to help the person living with ADHD find a more meaningful life through understanding ADHD and then making the necessary adjustments to be more fulfilled, relaxed, calm, and confident. Because there are people who will not understand ADHD, who will feel like it's too much work to try and deal with it, it is important that you are rooted in your Superpowers, your strengths. It's important that you have compassion for yourself, first and foremost. Therefore, be armed with information. Be ready to educate the people around you. Point them to the research. We need to not be afraid to ask for what we need. ADHD is a real condition with real problems, real symptoms, and real challenges. It's not an excuse, nor a way to avoid responsibility.

Most importantly, having ADHD doesn't mean we can't have fulfilling and meaningful lives. It means doing work that is significant to us, and having deeply engaging relationships. It means utilizing our talents and abilities to express our highest selves, bolstering the areas that challenge us without shame, and without criticizing or blaming ourselves for being inadequate. It means accepting our condition and making the best of it.

Once we are rooted firmly in our strengths and clear about our values it's easier not to settle for a case of the BADs. Brain Attention Deficit does not define us. We have ferreted out our shame where it hides in the shadows and have driven it into the light of day. We have refused to be defined by existential guilt. We have recognized what it means to be a Ferrari and are bound for the Autobahn. We recognize that we may not do well in a standard educational setting, and are committed to finding ways to learn that are meaningful and effective for us; ways that lead to meaningful livelihoods. Instead of a traditional college or university, this might mean an apprenticeship, or it might mean designing video games online. Whatever your strengths, talents, abilities, and passions call you to - this is the path with Heart. This is why you are here. Even if it means you want to do something that everyone around you thinks is silly, impossible, or foolish. If Naveen Jain believed he could not start a company that provides commercial flight to the moon, he never would have founded Moon Express!

We challenge the stigma associated with ADHD and refuse to be held back or defined by it. We've learned to care deeply for ourselves and for the people around us. We take measures to deal with ADHD by seeking all available supports. If that support is not available, we have learned – and now practice – the first and most important element of the Triple A Threat: *Advocacy*. We have gotten past the f**k-its and have found ways to get what we need in order to stay connected to our inner optimism. We have hope and we act on it.

We may have explored the option of medications prescribed for ADHD to help with specific tasks and to address any mood issues that come about as the result of having ADHD. We've done this without masking or band-aiding our thoughts and feelings about having ADHD. We are facing our very real needs. While many of us effectively manage ADHD without meds,

we recognize that there are legitimate times when psychophar-
macology can be our friend. And at those times, we seek the
assistance of a medical doctor who actually has a competency in
working with ADHD, and is not receiving kickbacks or payoffs
from pharmaceutical companies. We trust and feel good about
working with someone who listens to us and takes our input
into consideration, leaving us feeling empowered in our relationship with ADHD.

We advocate, seek accommodation without shame, and take
action to work through barriers. We use the tools and techniques
that work for us. Maybe we incorporate some of the tools in this
book, such as making a map of intentions with the Self Center,
hanging out with our Internal Commitments, using The Daily
Page, and/or the Bucket or Chuck-it list to keep track of what
is important to us. Or maybe we use something else, or some
system we have created ourselves. We do our best not to beat
ourselves up for not getting everything done that we planned to.
We realize that most techniques and tools – as well as Executive
Function supports and scaffolds – have a shelf life. That shelf life
can vary from person to person, but because we are in love with
the novel, or the new, we likely need to change our systems regularly. We are always openly seeking and exploring new methods
and ideas to help get and stay organized. Remember stuff, not
lose track of time, and be prepared for snafus and setbacks that
creep up out of nowhere.

We do our best to be prepared for the unexpected. As we
know, this is no easy feat. In general, we struggle with transitions, but not so much when we're grounded in activities that ab-
sorb our attention. Hyper-focus is one of our Superpowers. The
label ADHD is inaccurate. We don't have a deficit of attention.
We are able to deeply focus on things that interest us. What many
have is a deficit of the ability to regulate our strong emotions.
That makes it hard to sit still and focus on things that don't make
sense to us. We don't see the point and get upset when we are
forced to do so.

When we're disrupted, many of us become quite upset, or
when something unexpected happens that interrupts our course
of activity, it can set us back - big time! So what to do? Invite it.
Expect it. Be ready for those snafus and hitches. Nothing ever
quite goes as expected! We learn to laugh at set backs, just as we

can learn to flow, even through interruptions. We look for silver linings. By cultivating our inner optimism, we find the value in difficulty and challenge. We can see what is gained by enduring discomfort. Yes, we may require help from what the ADHD coaching world calls Body Doubles, people who act as an external scaffold to help us regulate and activate and support our executive function – that part of the brain that organizes, plans, and manages time. Sometimes in order to remember what's really important, we need a moment to breath, reset, and re-center. But we know that self-criticism and negativistic reflection don't help.

We ADHDers who live the Heartful path have discovered our Superpowers are our strengths *developed*. We've been able to develop what we're good at. We know what it feels like to be valued for what we have to offer. Our value is recognized and reflected by those around us. When we feel bogged down it's hard to see our strengths. When we get down on ourselves we find a way put the whip down, close our eyes, put on some music, smile, dance, and laugh. We've learned that if we aren't willing to do that, we're likely in the grip of a negativistic core belief. We need to wriggle our way out of those and find our way back to a clear vision of our strengths. So, whether we are really good at badminton, bocce ball, or car mechanics, we need to remember to connect with an environment or context where we can combine what we're good at with what we love in a way that the world needs. And we need positive reflection for these deliberate challenges.

We have come to realize that there is pretty much always less time than we think there is. We make decisions about managing our schedule using either digital or electronic means and might use primary colors – red, blue, yellow – to identify our values in the Time/Values audit. We might use an analog method of doing this. In other words a paper planner, a pencil, and an eraser. Old school! Or we might consider using Jessica McCabe's *Time-Spensive* worksheet to help determine if an activity or project is something we can afford to undertake. We take the time to figure out what is really important to us, block out time, ensuring we've established enough room in our schedule to adequately devote to what we've deemed important.

The Heartful path involves using tools and techniques to feel better. We've learned how ADHD can lead to depression and anxiety. We've learned to use tools like deep breathing, meditation, *Pronking*, and physical exercise as a means to ground. We've learned how to manage our energy. We recognized that food is mood, and that blood sugar regulation can have a significant impact on our ability to focus, control impulses, and remain still when we need to. We've explored the role of assessing food, fitness, and finance to ground and orient. We make efforts toward getting enough sleep, eating in a way that supports focus, stimulate our bodies in a way that produces feel good chemicals that sustain focus. Using Heartfulness we pay attention to how it feels to be with the people we are close to. Do the people we *choose* to hang out with enhance or diminish our your sense of Self? We use Heartful tools, such as a Gratitude Practice, or the Heartfulness Meditation to process through any negative feelings we might have about the people we have to interact with. This might include family members, co-workers, bosses or supervisors who annoy and irritate. I call these folks our *Petty Tyrants*.

We use physical exercise, Heartfulness meditation, reframing, and Pronking to work with our low frustration tolerance and angry outbursts. We might utilize *cognitive-behavioral triangles* to better understand the relationship between how we feel, what we do, and what we think. We are able to catch our *stinkin' thinkin'* and use practices such as *journaling, Teflon/Velcro affirmations*, and *WOOP* to change our denser feeling state, and negativistic thinking and emotional orientation. We increase our *experiential affluence*.

Once we have learned to live on purpose, we have likely figured out ways to augment our environment to help us do things in a way that produces better results. We've learned about conditions such as *Irlen Syndrome* and *HSP*. We've found ways to augment our personal world to improve the way we process external stimuli such as light and sound. By dimming light and reducing or changing sound levels our sympathetic nervous system is better able to work, and able to process both eustress and distress without nervous system blow-out or burn-out. This avoids shutting down, withdrawing, or reacting with extreme agitation. Many find that activities such as cooking and gardening can be quite grounding. For children, physical contact and augmented light and sound can be the difference between screaming our heads off and sleeping like a baby.

People with ADHD are often creative, ingenious, and re-sourceful. We frequently discover our own ways to adapt to the world around us, finding ways, means, and methods that are unique, individualized, awe inspiring, and strangely effective. There's a method to what might seem to others to be madness. We often create our own systems and operate outside of convention.

Some think that when people lived as nomadic tribes that we were scouts who went out ahead of the tribe to test things out to see if they were safe, reporting back from the edges of the unknown. With our heightened senses, unusual perspective, and ability to think on our feet, we now need to find roles that utilize and harness our strengths and highlight our keen abilities, talents, and skills. Like the ugly duckling who discovers he's a swan, ADHDers need recognition, knowledge, an environment that is a good fit, scaffolding, and a reason – a motivational buy in. We each need to find our own way to our version of the Autobahn. Together, with Heartful support, we can discover our Superpowers. We are visionaries. We are tomorrow people living in yesterday's world. Many of us may be the proverbial scouts for the human condition, informing human evolution of what's coming, and creating systems to help us gain a better under-standing of a world that is changing rapidly and exponentially.

Remember that life is an experiment. Stay open. Stay clear. Stay curious!

KEY POINTS

- Living with ADHD does not mean we have to live in a demoralized state.

- Challenging the stigma associated with ADHD is essential to claiming our strengths and moving toward using our Superpowers.

- Utilizing exercises such as *Pronking* and *Teflon/Velcro affirmations* can make the difference between feeling demoralized and living meaningful lives with ADHD.

- Making changes in our environment can significantly improve our experience and ability to work within the parameters of having ADHD.

- A Heartful Strength Based approach to living with ADHD. People with ADHD are often creative, ingenuous, and resourceful.

notes

_____

_____

_____

_____

_____

_____

_____

_____

_____

_____

_____

_____

_____

_____

_____

_____

_____

notes

Made in the USA
San Bernardino, CA
02 November 2018